THE HOPE OF ISRAEL: WHAT IS IT?

BY

PHILIP MAURO

"Not giving heed to Jewish fables" – *Titus 1:14*

ORIGINALLY PUBLISHED 1922

REPRINTED 2014

ISBN 978-1499525908

Ravenbrook Publishers

A subsidiary of
Shenandoah Bible Ministries

www.Ravenbrook.org

www.Shenbible.org

CONTENTS

Publisher's Forward   5

Forward   9

The Nature and Importance of the Question   11

How are the O.T. Prophecies of Blessing to Israel to be   15
    Interpreted?

How the O.T. Prophecies concerning Israel were Interpreted   24
    by Paul

What the Fathers of Israel were Looking for   30

God's Warnings through Moses to His Earthly People   34

God's Warnings through Moses *(Continued)*   47

God's Promises to the Children of Israel Fulfilled by Joshua   53

Salvation in Zion: The Sure Mercies of David   64

The Travail of Zion   70

The New Covenant   78

Ezekiel's Prophecies: Doom of Jerusalem, The Branch, the   85
    Shepherd of Israel, Valley of Death

Ezekiel's Temple; Waters Flowing from the House; Where   91
    Did the Spirit Descend at Pentecost?

What the N.T. Teaches as to Future Mercies for the Jews   109

"The Hope of the Gospel" – Christ's Personal Teaching   121

Other N.T. Passages on the Future of Israel   132

Where is the Promise of His Coming?   144

"The Election hath Obtained it" – Hath God Cast Away His People?   154

Building Again the Tabernacle of David   166

Shall Israel Be Restored as a Nation?   181

Concerning the Millennium   189

About the Author   205

PUBLISHER'S FORWARD

Almost forty years ago I cut my theological eyeteeth on the Puritans and received a solid, Biblical foundation that has served me well over the past decades of studying the Bible. About twenty-five years ago, after getting my theological degrees, I put all other books aside, put my Bible on the desk, and began a new phase in my learning program. I started out from scratch to learn what the message of the Bible is, told in God's own words.

In effect, I simply ignored everything that was being written in the field of Biblical studies during the twentieth century. Sometimes we have to do that, because the clamor of voices insisting to be heard are too often contradictory, inadequate, and confusing. When the experts can't agree on the basic issues, it's time to turn to the only source of Truth and listen for a change.

My method was to start with the simple truths and master them, then trace the connections that the Bible makes between them, and from there start putting together a network of the doctrines as they arranged themselves before me. It took about twenty years of studying both Old and New Testaments before I started seeing the *big picture* of the entire Bible. But I received a great deal of encouragement during the process of studying by the fact that different truths from all over the Bible *meshed together* and formed a Biblical system that is coherent and integrated. Once I managed to work it all out, and write my own version of a Biblical Theology, I finally turned to the field to see what others have been coming up with during the last century. What I discovered was that I seem to be seeing things in the Bible that others aren't talking about at all.

Leaving the crowd behind and going on alone can be fraught with dangers; many have fallen into error, even heresy, by ignoring or running contrary to solid Church tradition. That's the reason we have "multiple prophets" in the Church – to make sure there are no errant loners coming up with "unique" but wrong-headed doctrines. On the other hand, I firmly believe that a Christian needs only the

Bible, and the Spirit revealing the truth, in order to truly and sufficiently understand God's Message to mankind. Teachers and preachers *are* a necessary function in Christ's Church, but what they provide is a solid foundation, training, and the necessary discipline for the rest of us to carry on our own studies.

So I have always been on the lookout for someone else who would confirm that I'm on the right track with my studies. And that's where Philip Mauro comes into the picture. I have been surrounded for so long by both leaders and laymen who have never heard the idea that Israel's hope is nothing less than the Gospel of Christ. So imagine my surprise when I read these passages in Mauro's book:

> *Thus we find that the very last hope of mercy that is held out through Moses to that "disobedient and gainsaying people," to whom God says "I have stretched out my hands all the day long," is the "one hope" of the gospel of Christ.*

> *The essence of all this, stated in the fewest words, is that "this commandment which" – Moses said – "I command thee this day," and which was to be brought "very nigh" unto them, was to hear and obey the gospel of Christ.*

In fact his entire argument can be summed up in this way: *it's a serious mistake to think that the faithful Jews in the Old Testament were hoping for anything less than the spiritual Kingdom of Christ that we Christians are hoping for.* And since Mauro had just extricated himself from Dispensationalism, he makes the point plain, over and over, that anybody who believes that the Jews (past or future) are going to receive a physical fulfillment of the Old Testament promises is *just as much in error as were the Pharisees in Jesus' day*, who rejected outright the Lord's efforts to turn them in a spiritual direction.

This is the very heart of the message that I've been laboring to make plain in my own work over the last few years. If there's a difference between my work and Mauro's, it would be that I've worked out the *details* of the Old Testament system that correspond to our faith in Christ, whereas Mauro *proves* (he was a gifted lawyer and nobody to be trifled with in court!) that the hope of the Old and New systems is the same.

What was even more astonishing to me was to find Mauro turning to the Apostles for his hermeneutical methodology.

Paul quotes from this scripture (Deut. 30:11-14) and says that Moses was referring there to "the word of faith which we preach," that is, the gospel; and he declares the inner meaning of these words of Moses to be, "That if thou shalt confess with thy mouth the Lord Jesus" – Moses had said "in thy mouth and in thy heart" – "and shalt believe in thine heart that God hath raised him from the dead, thou shalt be saved" (Rom. 10:9). And the apostle goes on to say that the promise was not for penitent Jews only, but for all men: "For there is no difference between the Jew and the Greek; for whosoever shall call on the name of the Lord shall be saved" (vv. 12, 13).

Hardly any scholar in our current day does this! They are so afraid of "spiritualizing" the text that they insist on interpreting Moses and other Old Testament prophets solely in light of their ancient historical context. On the contrary, as Mauro points out again and again, the Apostles *knew* (by the Holy Spirit's revelation) exactly what Moses was thinking and referring to. Instead of ignoring the Apostles, we should be turning to them for the definitive hermeneutics of the Old Testament. I thought I was alone in insisting on this concept; but Mauro, with the lawyer's keen scent for the clinching argument, makes escape from the obvious impossible.

Whatever your views may be on eschatology, you must first reckon with Mauro's argument. When he shows conclusively that the Jewish hope has always been, and always will be, our spiritual Gospel, that decisively affects one's understanding of the end times and what can or can't happen. It's not good enough to respond by saying, "I don't believe it!" The lawyer has presented his case, and now you must satisfy the court that your case disproves his and successfully replaces his. Nothing less will do.

No doubt there have been others in the last hundred or so years who have taught these fundamental concepts of Biblical studies (the Lord *will* maintain his 7000!), but I doubt that few of them have had the mental and theological acumen to go right to the heart of the matter as Mauro does, and present it in such a near-flawless form.

Dr. Charles Vogan, May 2014

Note from the Publisher:

Since this text was scanned from the original, it may still contain a few spelling and typographical errors (though we have searched for them diligently!). Please let us know if you should find any errors of such nature, and we will correct future printings. We have chosen to retain Mauro's older-style spelling.

FORWARD

NOT GIVING HEED TO JEWISH FABLES *(Titus 1:14)*

Jewish fables (literally, *myths*) are no new thing. Paul has plainly warned the household of faith not to give heed thereto. He has not given us a list of those grievous heresies; but it is well known that the one that was most fondly cherished, and that constituted the gravest menace to the truth of the gospel, was the notion that the leading purpose of the mission of the coming Messiah would be the reconstitution of the Jewish nation and its elevation to the highest pinnacle of earthly dominion and glory; for that fatuous doctrine was the cornerstone of orthodox Judaism in Paul's day; and because of his sturdy opposition to it he was persecuted, his enemies plotted to take his life, and he was sent a prisoner to Rome. No wonder that, during the term of his imprisonment there, he wrote to Titus his plain-spoken warning against "Jewish fables."

Such being the case, we question if there be anything in all the long history of Christianity that is more difficult to account for than the fact that that particular fable, concerning the purpose of Christ's mission to the Jewish people, has become the central feature of a system of doctrine which, in this 20th century of our era, has found numerous and zealous advocates amongst orthodox Christians. In view of this extraordinary phenomenon, it surely behooves those who take the Holy Scriptures for their guide and instructor in all matters of faith and doctrine, to search them with the utmost care "whether these things be so." This present volume is the result of a painstaking investigation of that important question.

The investigation of that question leads inevitably to the subject of the Millennium; and it is believed the reader will find, in the last chapter of the present volume, something fresh upon that subject of perennial interest. Enough at this point to say that, as the author now sees it, the great question concerning the Millennium is not *When?* but *Where?*

9

CHAPTER I

THE NATURE AND IMPORTANCE OF THE QUESTION

The writer seeks, at the very outset of this study, to impress the reader with the immense importance of the question we are about to examine.

It is not merely a question of the true explanation of prophecies concerning the Jews, the Gentiles and of the Church of God, however so interesting and important these may be, for one may entertain mistaken ideas as to such matters without harmful consequences. But it is far otherwise with the question discussed in this volume; *for the truth concerning the gospel of Christ and the salvation of man is involved in it.* And specially, the work of evangelization of the Jews (which, in the opinion of many, including the present writer, the coming of the Lord awaits) is vitally affected by it.

What lies directly in the path of our present inquiry is a system of doctrine which, though of recent origin, is now accepted amongst strictly orthodox Christians, "Fundamentalists", according to which doctrinal system the promise of God to Israel through their prophets was that the coming Messiah would restore the earthly kingdom to Israel, would give it a glory far surpassing that of the days of David and Solomon, and would exalt the Jewish nation to the place of supremacy over the nations of the world. The leading authority for this new system of teaching states it thus: *"When Christ appeared to the Jewish people, the next thing in the order of revelation as it then stood should have been the setting up of the Davidic kingdom"* (*Scofield Ref. Bible*).

We propose in the present volume to bring this radical statement to the test of Scripture; for it is subversive of the Christian faith, in that it removes the sacrifice of the Lamb of God from its central place in God's eternal plan (Rev 13:8).

It cannot be that those who accept this radical doctrine realize what is involved in it. It is easy for the writer to believe this, because

11

he himself at one time accepted that doctrine without the faintest idea that it involved the denial of important truth. But in course of time, after prolonged study of the Word of God, he was compelled to acknowledge, upon the testimony of the New Testament Scriptures (particularly that of the apostle Paul) that, not only is the doctrine under consideration directly contrary to the Scriptures, but it is the setting up, for the benefit of a future generation of Jews, *of another hope*, different from the "one hope" of the gospel of Christ; that, in other words it is "another gospel," the very thing against which Paul utters that tremendously solemn warning of Galatians 1:8,9.

Because of this, and because also of the great benefits that have followed the writer's deliverance from the "strange" doctrine referred to above, he deems it a duty to all the household of faith to bring to their attention, by every available means, the true teaching of the Bible touching the future of the Jewish people. It is with a view to the performance of that duty that these pages are written.

What then *is* the true and biblical "Hope of Israel"? To obtain a full answer to this question it is necessary that we search the Scriptures from beginning to end. But in order merely that we may have in mind a general idea of the answer while we pursue our study, it will suffice to refer to a few incidents in Paul's ministry, as recorded in the last chapters of Acts.

The subject is very prominent there, and indeed it was because of Paul's views and his preaching in regard thereto that he was furiously persecuted by the Jews, and was finally sent in chains to Rome. For we have his own testimony to "the chief of the Jews" at Rome, to whom, when he had called them together, he said: "For this cause therefore have I called for you, to see you and to speak with you; because that, for *the hope of Israel* I am bound with this chain" (Acts 28:17-20).

Inasmuch as what Paul had been preaching, both to the Jews and also to the Gentiles, was the gospel of Jesus Christ, and nothing else, it follows that the true "hope of Israel" is an essential part of that gospel; and therefore it is a matter regarding which we cannot afford to be mistaken.

12

The above quoted statement of Paul to the Jewish leaders at the imperial city is very illuminating. It shows, to begin with, that, whatever it was he had been preaching as "the hope of Israel," it was something *so contrary to the current Jewish notion thereof* that it caused the people to clamour for his death (Acts 22:22), and led to his being formally accused before the Roman Governor as "a pestilent fellow, and a mover of sedition among all the Jews throughout the world" (Id. 24:5). Had he been preaching what the Jews themselves believed to be, and what their rabbis had given them as, the true interpretation of the prophecies (namely, that God's promise to Israel was a kingdom of earthly character which should have dominion over all the world) they would have heard him with intense satisfaction. But what Paul and all the apostles preached was, that what God had promised afore by His prophets in the Holy Scriptures was a kingdom over which Jesus Christ of the seed of David should reign in *resurrection*, a kingdom which flesh and blood *cannot inherit*, a kingdom which does *not* clash with the duly constituted governments of this world, and one into which the Gentiles are called *upon terms of perfect equality* with Jews (Acts 13:23, 34; Acts 17:2,3,7; Rom. 1:1-4; 14:17; 1 Cor. 15:50; 1 Pet. 1:12; cf. Luke 24:26).

Thus the teaching of Christ and His apostles in respect to the vitally important subject of the Kingdom of God, the hope of Israel, came into violent collision with that of the leaders of Israel; and because of this *He* was crucified and *they* were persecuted.

It was not a question then, any more than it is a question now, whether or not the prophets of Israel were the mouthpieces of God; for the Jewish rabbis, as well as Christ and His apostles, held firmly to the full inspiration of "the scriptures of the prophets." It was solely a question then, as it is solely a question now, as to *how those prophecies are to be understood* – a question of *interpretation*. The Jewish teachers understood the scriptures, and still interpret them, in what is now (wrongly) called the "literal" sense (i.e. that "Israel" is an earthly people, "Zion" an earthly locality, "Christ" an earthly conqueror, like David, etc., etc.); but Paul declared, when speaking of Jesus Christ in one of their synagogues, that it was "because they knew Him not, nor yet *the voices of the prophets* which are read every Sabbath day, that they *have* fulfilled them in condemning *Him*" (Acts 13:27).

And now, in concluding this preliminary chapter, let me impress it upon the reader's mind that the choice presented to orthodox Christians today as to the interpretation of the prophecies concerning "the hope of Israel" lies between that held by the Jews of those days and that for which Christ was crucified and Paul was sent in chains to Rome. This will be clearly seen by all who consider, with open minds, the proofs given below.

The question of the "literal" interpretation of the O.T. prophecies will be discussed in the next chapter.

CHAPTER II

HOW ARE THE O.T. PROPHECIES OF BLESSING TO ISRAEL TO BE INTERPRETED?

The main purpose of the present chapter is to bring clearly to view the important truth that in Scripture the contrast is not between the *spiritual* and the *literal*, but between the *spiritual* and *natural*; for a passage of Scripture may refer, when taken "literally," either to "that which is *natural*" or to "that which is spiritual." In other words, the literal interpretation may call for a thing which exists in the realm of nature, or for the counterpart of that thing which exists in the realm of spiritual realities (1 Cor. 15:46). It is of the utmost importance that this be understood; for the advocates of modern dispensationalism have wrought confusion, and have succeeded in giving plausibility to many misinterpretations of Scripture, by first taking for granted (erroneously, as will be herein shown) that a "literal" interpretation necessarily calls for something *material* or *natural*, and by then insisting strenuously that all prophecies which refer to *Israel, Jerusalem, Zion*, etc., should be interpreted "literally." It will not be difficult to show that this is a thoroughly unsound principle of interpretation, that it is based upon a false premise, and that its application has made havoc of many prophecies.

For example, those expositors who think the Bible teaches us to expect hereafter a millennium of earthly bliss, a golden age of world-wide peace and plenty, during which the Jewish nation will be reconstituted and will have the place of headship over a world occupied by God-fearing and peace-loving Gentiles, base that expectation upon certain Old Testament prophecies which, they think, are to be fulfilled "literally"; and since they cannot possibly be fulfilled in that manner during this era of the Gospel, there must needs be an age to come of an entirely different character from this day of gospel salvation.

This argument, however, is utterly fallacious, because it is based upon a false premise. Those who make use of it take for granted that in order to interpret a prophecy "literally" its fulfillment must be located in the realm of nature, and not in the *spiritual* [eternal] realm. Thus they assume that the "literal" interpretation is in contrast with the "spiritual" interpretation thereof; and they denounce and repudiate what they refer to disparagingly as "the *spiritualizing*" of the prophecies.

Undoubtedly our natural bias is in favor of the so-called "literal" interpretation of the prophecies in question; for to the natural man the things that are seen are the *real* things; and to that view we are disposed to cling tenaciously, notwithstanding the plain teaching of the New Testament that the seen things are but the fleeting shadows of things unseen, the latter being the spiritual and eternal *realities* with which the promises of future blessing have mainly to do. For the New Testament Scriptures state, in most unambiguous language, that "the seed of Abraham," to whom "*all* the promises of God" belong, are those who believe the gospel of Jesus Christ (Gal. 3:7, 29; 2 Cor. 1:20). Further, in the New Testament it is plainly revealed that, even as "Abraham had *two* sons" (which might make it uncertain whether the descendants of Ishmael or those of Isaac were to inherit the promises) so likewise there is a *natural* "Israel," "Zion" and "Jerusalem" and also a *spiritual counterpart* of each; and that just as Ishmael preceded in time the true heir (though eventually he was to be "cast out" and not to be "heir with the son of the free woman") even so the natural *Israel, Zion,* and *Jerusalem* preceded the respective spiritual realities to which those names properly belong. For God's invariable order of procedure, in the working out of His eternal purposes, is "*first* – that which is *natural*, and afterward that which is *spiritual*" (1 Cor. 15:46).

If, therefore, an O.T. prophecy of blessing, intended for the true Israel (that "holy nation" of 1 Pet. 2:9), be interpreted as applying to "Israel after the flesh," the interpretation is not "literal" (i.e., according to the letter) except in the sense in which "the *letter* killeth, but the spirit giveth life" (2 Cor. 3:6); for obviously in this case the "literal" interpretation destroys the prophecy completely. And it is specially to be noted that, in the passage from which this Scripture is quoted, Paul is explaining the great differences between the Old Covenant (which was of *the letter*) and the New Covenant (of *the Spirit*); and, moreover, he is comparing the ministry of Moses, which had to do with things that are seen (an earthly

16

sanctuary and its vessels of service, animal sacrifices, etc.), with the ministry of himself and others whom God had made "able ministers of the New Covenant; *not of the letter*, but of *the spirit*." Also it should be noted that the apostle there speaks of the Old Covenant (under which promises were made to the *natural* Israel) as "*that which is done away*"; whereas the New Covenant is "that which *remaineth*," that is, abideth eternally (v. 11).

From this Scripture alone it is evident (and the same truth is set forth at greater length in Gal. 4:21-31 and Hebrews Chapters VIII-X) that all future promises of glory and blessing for Israel and Zion must belong to the true Israel and the heavenly Zion. And, in this very passage, we are admonished to "look not at the things which are seen, but at the things which are not seen" (4:18); which admonition, however, is habitually disregarded in the interpretation of prophecies relating to these very subjects.

We ask the reader specially to note that in the above quoted passage, the apostle speaks of the old covenant as "that which *is* done away" (v. 11), "that which is abolished" (v. 13). This shows that the old covenant, under which the earthly nation of Israel had been constituted, was already, in Paul's day, a thing of the past.

Evidently then our difficulty in understanding prophecies of the class referred to above is due to our lack of faith and our spiritual dullness. For, in respect to the things which are not seen, *faith* takes the place of *sight*; for faith has to so solely with things not visible to the natural eye; and hope likewise, for "hope that is seen is not hope" (Rom. 8:24). Wherefore it is written that, "faith is the *substance of things hoped for*, the evidence of things *not seen*"; and "through faith we understand" (Heb. 11:1,3).

Hence, to *understand* the prophecies it is necessary, and vitally necessary, that we *believe* the revelations of the New Testament; that we accept as "literally" true that there is now, at this present time, *a realm of spiritual realities*, into which our risen Lord is actually entered, and *we in Him*; that "the *substance* of things hoped for" is *there*, not here; and specially that God's purposes concerning His City, Temple and People are being fulfilled *at this very time*, in that spiritual realm, though the natural eye cannot see what is going on there.

The writer of these lines can testify from experience that, by the simple process of believing what is written in the New Testament concerning the *actual present existence*, among the things not seen, of the true Zion, of the city of the living God the heavenly Jerusalem, of the holy nation which is a royal priesthood, and of other spiritual realities, the main difficulty in the understanding of the Old Testament prophecies which speak of a glorified state of the things named above, vanishes away.

AN ILLUSTRATION FROM ZECHARIAH

Zechariah is one of the books that is frequently referred to as containing prophecies which await a "literal" fulfillment in a future dispensation.

Zechariah, with Haggai, prophesied during the rebuilding of Jerusalem and the temple, after the return from Babylon of some of the deported Israelites; at which time "the elders of the Jews builded and they prospered through the prophesying of Haggai the prophet and Zechariah the son of Iddo" (Ezra 6:14). But, as all are agreed, the prophet looks beyond what those men were building, to a temple and a city that were to be far more glorious. He records the word of the Lord concerning Zion: "For, lo I come, and I will dwell in the midst of thee, saith the Lord. And many nations shall be joined to the Lord *in that day* and shall be My people; and I will dwell in the midst of thee" (2:10,11). And the prophet goes on to speak of a priest, Joshua, who was clothed at first with filthy garments, but to whom it was said, "Behold, I have caused thine iniquity to pass from thee, and I will clothe the with change of raiment" (3:3,4). This Joshua and his fellows were to be "men wondered at; for, behold, I will bring forth my servant the Branch. For behold the stone that I have laid before Joshua" (vv. 8,9).

There is no difficulty in recognizing in this passage a prophecy of the coming of Christ as the Branch of Jehovah and as the Foundation Stone of the true Temple of God; for Peter (quoting a similar prophecy by Isaiah) writes to those who have been "redeemed... by the precious blood of Christ," saying:

18

"Wherefore also it is contained in the Scripture, Behold I lay in Sion a chief corner stone, elect, precious"; and he had just said in the preceding verse, "Ye also, as living stones are [being] built up, a *spiritual* house, an holy priesthood" – as typified by Joshua's change of garments – "to offer up *spiritual* sacrifices" (1 Pet. 2:5,6). Thus by Peter's application of the prophecy we are given plainly to understand that it relates to "spiritual" things, and that it is now being fulfilled in the spiritual realm.

It will greatly help us in our efforts to understand the class of prophecies above referred to, if we give due heed to the facts stated in the above quotation from Peter (and stated also in Hebrews 12:22-24, and in the Epistle to the Ephesians as pointed out below) that God's *"spiritual house"* is in course of erection *now*, that it is being built "in Sion", and that the believers in Jesus Christ are "living stones" therein, and are also a "royal priesthood."

Zechariah refers again (6:12-15) to "the Man whose name is The BRANCH," and who "shall build the temple of the Lord"; and says of Him that "He shall bear the glory, and He shall sit and rule upon His throne; and He shall be a priest upon His throne." None will dispute, in the light of New Testament Scriptures, that this prophecy is being fulfilled *now* (Heb. 2:9; 8:1, etc.). And the prophet goes on to say that crowns shall be given also to certain men, whom he names, and that "they that are *far off*" (a scriptural designation of Gentiles, see Acts 2:39 and Eph 2:13), "shall come and build in the temple of the Lord."

Furthermore, in Zechariah 9:9 we have the familiar passage: "Rejoice greatly, O daughter of Zion... behold, thy King cometh unto thee"; and we know to a certainty, from Luke 19:38, that that prophecy was fulfilled when Christ came to Jerusalem to die for our salvation.

In Zechariah 13:7-9 the atoning death of Christ is foretold in the words, "Awake, O sword, against My Shepherd, and against the Man that is My Fellow, saith the Lord of hosts. Smite the Shepherd, and the sheep shall be scattered" (See Matt. 26:31). And what was to follow as regards the Jewish people is foretold in these words: "And it shall come to pass that in all the land, saith the Lord, two parts shall be *cut off*, and die; but the third part shall be left therein." And in agreement with this, the two great parties, the Pharisees and the Sadducees, were "cut off"; but a third part, *the disciples of Christ*, were left. And as to these, the prophecy goes on to say: "And I will bring the third part through the fire and will refine them as silver is refined" (See 1 Pet. 1:6 and 4:12); "they shall call on My Name and I will hear them. I will say, It is *My people*; and they shall say, The Lord is My God" (See Rom. 11:1,2).

Moreover, the apostle Paul declares the same truth concerning the building of God's true temple *now* as declared by Peter. He makes known that those who believe in Jesus Christ are even now "quickened together with Christ, – and raised up together, and made to *sit* together [*i.e. on thrones*] in heavenly places [Zion] in Christ Jesus" (Eph. 2:5,6); which plainly declares that we live and reign with Christ even now. This indeed is not perceived with the natural eye or realized in our conscious experience. Nevertheless it is true, and this truth is developed in Chapter XX of this volume.

And furthermore, in the immediate context, Paul also declares the companion truth revealed by Peter, namely that the saints of this era, Gentiles as well as Jews, and being "built upon the foundation of the apostles and prophets, Jesus Christ Himself being the chief corner stone; in whom all the building, fitly framed together, groweth into *an holy temple* in the Lord" (vv. 20, 21).

The expression "in that day" occurs about twenty times in the book of Zechariah; and, as a judicious commentator says, "It is a synonym for the great Messianic hope." The first of these occurrences we have quoted, "And many nations shall be joined unto the Lord *in that day*" (2:11). What was "*that* day", then, is *this* day *now*, for "*now* is the day of salvation"; and "all the prophets from Samuel... as many as have spoken, have likewise foretold of *these* days" (Acts 3:24). And so, when Zechariah says (13:1) "*In that day* there shall be a fountain opened to the house of David and to the inhabitants of Jerusalem for sin and for uncleaness," we understand clearly that he is foretelling the cross of Christ; as very plainly appears from verse 7, "Awake, O sword, against My Shepherd, and against the Man that is My Fellow, saith the Lord of hosts; smite the Shepherd, and the sheep shall be scattered." Further reference to the prophecies of Zechariah will be found in Chapter X, *The New Covenant*.

Enough has been said, however, to make evident that the prophecies of Zechariah referred to above, and hence other prophecies of like character as well, relate to things spiritual and have their fulfillment in this present era of grace.

But it will be profitable to follow a little further the subject of the building of God's true temple. So we recall that, at our Lord's first visit to Jerusalem, when He had driven the traffickers out of the temple which Herod had built and which was one of the wonders of the world; and when the onlookers demanded of Him what sign He could give in proof of his authority to do those things, He answered and said unto them, *"Destroy this temple, and in three days I will raise it up"* (John 2:19). The Jews understood this "literally"; that is to say, they took it as applying to that building of material stones which stood on Mt. Moriah; and had the record stopped there, it would doubtless be insisted by some in our day that that great edifice, which has been meanwhile destroyed so completely that not one stone remains upon another, is to be miraculously restored in the coming millennium. But, to the end that we should not be misled and also *that we might have a key to the interpretation of prophetic utterances of this sort*, the Spirit caused John to insert the explanatory note: "But He spake of *the Temple of His Body.*"

This is just one of the many, seemingly casual, indications scattered throughout the Scriptures, that God's promises are to be fulfilled and His purposes are to be accomplished *in the resurrection*; that is to say, in the new creation.

Again, at a subsequent visit to Jerusalem, at the season of one of the feasts, "In the last day, that great day of the feast, Jesus stood and cried saying, If any man thirst, let him come to Me and drink, he that believeth on Me, as the Scripture hath said, out of his belly shall flow rivers of living water" (John 7:37,38). We might well wonder what would have been made of this saying by those who insist upon "literal" interpretations, had it been left unexplained; and therefore we should be thankful indeed for the added words, "But this spake He *of the Spirit*, which they that believe on Him should receive; for the Holy Ghost was not yet given; because that Jesus was not yet

21

glorified." Those words put beyond all uncertainty the meaning of the phrase "living water," as used, for example, in Zechariah 14:8, "And it shall be *in that day* that *living waters* shall go out from Jerusalem; half of them toward the former (or eastern, *marg.*) sea [the Caspian], and half of them towards the hinder sea" [the Mediterranean] – in other words, both eastward and westward – "in summer and in winter it shall be" – that is, all the year round.

In the light of John's explanation, we understand, therefore, that out Lord was foretelling, not some extraordinary *physical* phenomenon, which was to happen in a far off millennial age, but the then approaching era of the Holy Spirit, when there was to be an outflow of the gospel, "with the Holy Ghost sent down from heaven" (1 Pet. 1:12), both eastward and westward from Jerusalem. Thus both the place whence (Jerusalem) and the time when ("in that day") those living waters were to begin to flow out into all the world, both summer and winter, are plainly foretold in Zechariah's prophecy. Further explanations of the prophecies concerning the outflow of living waters from the Temple at Jerusalem will be found below (Chapter XIII) in connection with a discussion of Ezekiel's temple and of the question, *Where did the Spirit descend at Pentecost?*

And again let it be noted that these explanations put us in possession of the general principle upon which all prophecies of the same sort should be interpreted. They harmonize fully with all other indications contained in the Scriptures; making it abundantly plain that all the prophecies of future glory and blessing for Israel, Zion, and Jerusalem, pertain to that "holy nation" (1 Peter 1:9) "the Israel of God" (Gal. 6:16), and to that heavenly "Mount Sion," and to "the city of the living God, the *heavenly* Jerusalem," to which we already "*are* come" (Heb 12:22.).

Therefore, for the above, and for other reasons set forth elsewhere in this volume, the writer reaches the conclusion that we are to look for the fulfillment of the prophecies in question – not to another *age* than this, but – to another *locality*; namely, to that *spiritual* realm, which Paul designates "*the heavenlies*"; where our Lord is gone to prepare a place for us, where the true temple is now in course of erection, and where already exists "the Jerusalem which is above, which is the mother of us all" (Gal. 4:26).

The idea of a future "dispensation" for the fulfillment of prophecies on the earth, abounds in difficulties, and moreover it contradicts many passages of Scripture; whereas the idea of *another locality*, a spiritual and heavenly realm where those prophecies are in course of fulfillment *now*, is free from all difficulty, and has, moreover, the support of many N.T. Scriptures.

Concerning the now-existing realm of unseen things enough is said in the Scriptures to make known that it is a region of great activity; that the "principalities and powers" therein are numerous and mighty – angels and demons, good spirits and evil – and hence we must infer that there are happenings there which are of immense importance and significance. For example, we read: "There was a war in heaven. Michael and his angels fought against the dragon; and the dragon fought and his angels" (Rev. 12:7). Also, that "we wrestle not against flesh and blood, but against principalities, against powers, against the rulers of the darkness of this world, against spiritual wickedness in high places" (Eph. 6:12).

In this connection it were well to recall that the title of the last book of the Bible, "The Apocalypse," means *the unveiling*; that is to say, the taking away of the veil that normally separates the realm of spiritual things from that of natural things. That the title indicates that the visions described in the book of "Revelation" bring into view things and happenings in the spiritual realm, whereof, except for this unveiling, we should be wholly unaware. And when we come to Chapter XX, where is found the only reference in the Bible to the millennium – "the thousand years" – the language of the inspired writer makes it evident that the happenings of the millennium *are part of the history of the spirit realm*. This will be shown in the last chapter of this volume. It follows that all effort to find a place for those happenings in the history of this physical world, whether before or after the second advent, is utterly vain.

CHAPTER III

HOW THE O.T. PROPHECIES CONCERNING ISRAEL WERE INTERPRETED BY PAUL

We shall be the better prepared for an examination of the O.T. prophecies concerning "the hope of Israel" if we first observe how those prophecies were interpreted by the N.T. writers, especially Paul. Therefore we call attention at this point to a few N.T. passages.

When Porcius Festus remanded Paul for trial before King Herod Agrippa on the charges lodged against him by the Jews, and when the king had given the apostle leave to speak for himself, he said:

"And now I stand and am judged for *the hope of the promise made of God unto our fathers*; unto which promise our twelve tribes, instantly serving God day and night hope to come. For which hope's sake, King Agrippa, I am accused of the Jews" (Ac. 26:6, 7).

This is very definite. It proves that Paul, in preaching the gospel of Christ crucified and risen from the dead, was proclaiming to the people of Israel the fulfillment of God's promise to that people; a promise that had been made, not only to them through Moses and the prophets, but also directly to their fathers – Abraham, Isaac and Jacob. And this, be it noted, is in exact agreement with the testimony of Peter, who, writing to converted Jews of the dispersion and speaking of the prophets of Israel, said: "Unto whom it was revealed that, not unto themselves but unto us, they did minister *the things which are now reported unto you by them that have preached the gospel unto you*" (1 Pet. 1:10-12).

Paul's statement to King Agrippa further proves that this gospel-salvation, which he preached, was and had been the hope of every true Israelite – "all our *twelve tribes.*" Therefore the true hope of Israel was not, and is not, an earthly kingdom which some future generation of Jews, men of flesh and blood, are to inherit. Furthermore, the true Israel of God, as Paul himself had previously explained in his epistle to the Romans, is composed of *believing*

Israelites according to the flesh, with believing Gentiles added to them, forming one body, as represented by the olive-tree of Romans XI.

The above statement of Paul to King Agrippa also makes clear what he meant by saying: "Israel hath not obtained *that which he seeketh for*; but the election hath obtained it, and the rest were blinded" (Rom. 11:7). For the true hope and expectation of all Israel – "our twelve tribes" – *lay in the resurrection*, where the promise of the "sure mercies of David" was to be fulfilled (Acts 13:34). It matters not that, as individuals, they were nearly all "blinded" to it, and were looking for a kingdom of earthly grandeur, suited to their carnal ideas; for the truth of their own Scriptures was that the kingdom of God, which had been promised by their prophets, was a spiritual kingdom, to be realized in the resurrection of the dead, and to be entered only by those who are born again of the Word and Spirit of God.

The Lord Jesus Himself had given the same teaching concerning the Kingdom of heaven (or Kingdom of God, the two expressions being used by Him interchangeably). Thus He taught His disciples, saying, "Verily I say unto you, except ye be converted and become as little children, ye shall not enter into the *kingdom of heaven*" (Matt. 18:3); and He goes on to show that to enter into that kingdom is to "enter into life" (vv. 8-11). And this he followed up by declaring how hard it is for a rich man to enter into the kingdom (Matt. 19:16-26), calling it in one verse (23) "the kingdom *of heaven*," and in the next, "the kingdom *of God*." And He concluded the lesson by saying to those who had forsaken all and followed Him; "Verily I say unto you, that ye which have followed me, in the regeneration when the Son of man shall sit in the throne of His glory, ye shall also sit upon *twelve thrones, judging the twelve tribes of Israel*" (v. 28).

From this it appears that the "all Israel" of Scripture here designated as "the twelve tribes of Israel," is a *spiritual nation*; and that it shall come into its inheritance in the day of "glory," when the kingdom of God shall be manifested, and when Christ, who is now upon His Father's throne in heaven, shall occupy the throne of His glory.

Returning now to Paul's defense before King Agrippa, we note his concluding words:

"Having therefore obtained help of God, I continue unto this day, witnessing both to small and great, saying" – not a new thing, a mystery never before revealed, but – "*none other things than those which the prophets and Moses did say should come*" – not that Christ would restore earthly dominion to national Israel, as now is widely taught amongst Christians, but – "*that Christ should suffer*, and that He should be the first that should *rise from the dead*, and should show light unto *the people* [Israel] and to *the Gentiles*" (Ac. 26:22,23).

Here is clear proof that the gospel proclaims nothing that was not foretold by the prophets; for, as we know from Paul's teaching elsewhere, the "mystery" of the gospel was that believing *Gentiles* were to become "fellow citizens with the saints and of the household of God," being made "fellow heirs [with saved Jews] and of the same body, and partakers [with saved Jews] of His promise in Christ"; and that all this was to be accomplished "by [means of] the gospel" (Eph. 2:11-22; 3:6,9).

And the last quoted passage also proves that the predicted manifestation of light to the people of Israel and to the Gentiles was to come after the sufferings of the promised Messiah and his resurrection from the dead. Here we have the statement of an inspired apostle as to what was the order of revelation as it stood when Christ appeared to the Jewish people; – not "the setting up of the Davidic kingdom," as stated by the leading exponent of modern dispensationalism, but – the sufferings of Christ and His resurrection from the dead, followed by the showing of Gospel light to the Jew fist, and also to the Gentile. In other words, that "the next thing in the order of divine revelation" was precisely what came to pass.

By this it appears that Paul's statement as to what was "the next thing in the order of revelation as it then stood" flatly contradicts that of the *Scofield Reference Bible*, quoted above.

Likewise the apostle Peter, in a passage already quoted (1 Pet. 1:9-12), makes known what was "the next thing in the order of

26

divine revelation" as it then stood; namely, the "salvation" concerning which the prophets of Israel had enquired and searched diligently, searching what the Spirit of Christ, who was in them did signify when He testified beforehand *"the sufferings of Christ and the glories* [plural] *that should follow."*

We have referred in the preceding chapter to the fact that Paul, when he arrived in Rome, sent for the leading Jews of that city and declared to them that it was "for the hope of Israel" he had been brought thither in chains (Ac. 28:20). The next succeeding verses make evident that the hope of Israel was *the Kingdom of God* as Paul had preached it everywhere (Ac. 17:3, 7; 19:8; 20:25), and as he had expounded and defined it in his Epistle to the Romans (14:17). For the account in Acts 28 continues:

And when they had appointed him a day there came many to him to his lodging; to whom he expounded and testified *the Kingdom of God,* persuading them concerning Jesus both out of *the law of Moses* and out of *the prophets,* from morning till evening" (v. 23).

Inasmuch as those Jews were thoroughly indoctrinated with the then current Jewish teaching, it needed, of course, much exposition and persuasion, and the enlightenment of the Spirit of God besides, to make evident to them that what Moses and the prophets had foretold was a spiritual kingdom, which was to be established through the sufferings and death of the expected Messiah of Israel. But it is an extraordinary thing indeed that, after the truth in this regard has been clearly set forth in the N.T. Scriptures, and has been apprehended by successive generations of Christians for nineteen centuries, there should have arisen in these days a system of doctrine which takes for one of its foundation stones the very same error touching the true hope of Israel which turned Paul's fellow Israelites against him.

To those at Rome who "believed not" the things spoken by Paul, he used great plainness of speech, saying to them:

"Well spake the Holy Ghost by Esias the prophet unto our fathers, saying, Go unto this people, and say, Hearing ye hear and not understand; and seeing ye shall see and not perceive. For the heart of this people is waxed gross, and their ears are dull of hearing, and their eyes have they closed; lest they should see with their eyes, and hear with their ears, and understand with their heart, and should be converted, and I should heal them. Be it known therefore unto you that the *salvation of God* is sent unto the Gentiles and that they will hear it" (vv. 25-27).

By this it appears that *the hope of Israel, the kingdom of God* and *the salvation of God* are three different names for one and the same thing. And it also shows that a supernatural and punitive blindness *concerning the kingdom foretold by the prophets* had been laid upon the unbelieving part of the natural Israel, even as the same prophets had predicted; which blindness, as we learn from Romans 11:25, is to continue "until the fullness of the Gentiles be come in." But who can explain how it is that the very same error which Paul here denounced, and for the denouncing of which he suffered persecution and imprisonment, has found advocates among orthodox Christians of the twentieth century?

The Scriptures we have been reviewing make it plain that "the hope of Israel" was to be realized in the resurrection. Christ was to suffer, to die, and to rise again; He the first, and afterward they that are His (1 Cor. 15:23). There is no other hope for Israel, and never was. If the promise of God to Israel had been earthly dominion, or if that had been even a part of the promise, it is impossible that Paul should not have declared it on the occasions to which we have referred, and should not have spoken of it in his Epistles –especially Romans. Nor could he possibly in that case, have used the language we have quoted above.

There are indeed certain prophetic passages in the Old Testament which, apart from the light afforded by the New, might be taken as relating to "Israel after the flesh," and as foretelling the restoration, at some future day, of their national greatness; for there is in those passages no distinct reference to the resurrection. But that goes for nothing. For the natural intelligence could not possibly have discerned that Psalm 16 and Isaiah 55:3 were to be fulfilled in the resurrection. The Holy Spirit, however, by the apostle Peter, has given us to know that David, in the 16th Psalm, was foretelling that

God "would *raise up Christ* to sit on his throne" (Ac. 2:30, 31); and by the apostle Paul the same Spirit has made known that the broad promise of "the sure mercies of David" was to be fulfilled *in the resurrection of Christ from the dead* (Ac. 13:32-34).

The erroneous doctrine of the teachers of Israel which we have been discussing, was based upon an unspiritual interpretation of their own Scriptures; for "they knew not the voices of the prophets which were read every Sabbath day" (Ac. 13:27). That doctrine was fatal to everyone who received and clung to it; and also to the nation as a whole. Therefore, its revival amongst orthodox Christians in these days is a proper cause for serious misgivings.

CHAPTER IV

WHAT THE FATHERS OF ISRAEL WERE LOOKING FOR

"Faith is the substance of things hoped for"
(Hebrews 11:1)

We turn back now to the Old Testament Scriptures for the purpose of ascertaining what is foretold therein concerning the future of the Israelitic people, and particularly what, if any, indication they contain as to the restoration of their national greatness in a yet future day.

And first we direct our attention to the patriarchal era, in order to learn what it was that the fathers of Israel were taught of the Lord to anticipate for themselves and their posterity. This is the proper place to begin our inquiry; for we recall that when Paul was arraigned before King Herod Agrippa by his infuriated fellow countrymen, because he preached a hope for Israel radically different from that held and taught by them and their rabbis, he declared that he was "judged for *the hope of the promise made of God to our fathers.*" And he went on to say that God's promise to the fathers was the true hope of all Israel – "our twelve tribes" (Ac. 26:6,7).

It is written that "faith is the substance of things hoped for." If, therefore, we know what a man is *hoping for,* we know what he *believes.* "The *faith* of Jesus Christ" is that on which is founded "the *hope* of the gospel" (Col. 1:23); and there is just the "one hope" for all men (Eph. 4:4); because there is but *one* gospel (and never was, or will be, "another *gospel.*" Gal. 1:6-9). The hope of the gospel has ever been the coming of Him who should bruise the serpent's head, and who should be Himself "bruised" in the deadly conflict; Him who by death should destroy him, that had the power of death, the Devil.

It is fitting that the faith of Abraham should have a large space in the eleventh chapter of Hebrews; for Abraham is "the father of *all them that believe*" (Rom. 4:11). That chapter does not state what the gospel was that "God preached unto Abraham" (Gal. 3:8); but it tells what the effect thereof was upon his life and conduct, and what his hope was, that is, *what he was looking for*. It is recorded that –

> By faith he sojourned in the land of promise as in a strange (or foreign) country, dwelling in tents with Isaac and Jacob, *the heirs with him of the same promise*" (v. 9)

And verse 10 gives the explanation –

> "*For* he looked (lit. *was waiting for*) the (not *a*) city which hath foundations, whose Builder and Maker is God."

Mention is made also of Sarah's faith, which was also an important factor in the accomplishment of the purposes of God, and who is herself a type of that heavenly city upon which Abraham's hope was fixed...the "Jerusalem which is above, which is the mother of all" (Gal. 4:26). And further, it is expressly declared that Isaac and Jacob were co-heirs with Abraham of "*the same promise*" (v. 9). And then, concerning those four – Abraham, Isaac, Jacob and Sarah, to whom "the promises" were directly given, we have this illuminating testimony:

> "These all died in faith, not having received *the promises*, but having seen them afar off; and were persuaded [fully convinced] of them, and embraced them, and confessed that they were strangers and pilgrims *on the earth*. For they that say such things declare plainly that they *seek a country*. And truly, if they had been mindful of that country from whence they came out, they might have had opportunity to have returned. But now they *seek a better country*, that is, *an heavenly*: *wherefore God is not ashamed to be called their God; for He hath prepared for them a city*" (vv. 13-16).

This gives us clearly to know, *first* that "the promises" exerted a mighty influence over those to whom they were first given, (proving that their faith in what God had spoken was real and unwavering); and *second*, that the nature of the promises were such as to turn their thoughts *entirely away from the earth*, and to raise in their hearts the expectation of a country "better" than the very best of earth (showing that the promises themselves were *spiritual and heavenly in character*). For those promises had the effect of making even "the land of promise" itself to be to them as a foreign country. For while the land of Canaan was indeed promised to Abraham's natural seed, that promise never was "the hope of Israel." The hope of the gospel which God preached to Abraham was of such a nature that it caused him, and those who were "the heirs with him of the same promise," to declare themselves "strangers and pilgrims *on the earth*."

As will be more fully shown in subsequent Chapters, God's promise that He would bring Abraham's descendants into that land was punctually fulfilled. For it is recorded in the Book of Joshua that "the Lord gave unto Israel *all the land which he sware unto their fathers to give them, and they possessed it*, and dwelt therein... *There failed not ought of any good thing which the Lord hath spoken unto the house of Israel*" (Josh. 21:43-45). But the possession of that land by later generations was forfeited through disobedience, apostasy, and idolatry, even as Moses and Joshua foretold; and, in consequence of their complete repudiation of Jehovah their God, they were "plucked off the land" (Deut. 28:63,64; Joshua 12:13). And thus was fulfilled the prophetic "allegory" of Abraham's family history, according to which the bondwoman and her son, representing Israel after the flesh, were to be "cast out" (Gal. 4:30); which is the end of their history as a nation.

It was not until centuries of time had passed, not until faith had vanished from among the children of Israel, not until the true spiritual and eternal character of the promises had faded out of sight, and fleshly lusts had taken the place of heavenly hopes and longings, that there arose among the natural seed of Abraham the ruinous doctrine that "the hope of Israel" was an *earthly thing*. That doctrine was the product of degenerate times. It was tenaciously held and zealously propagated by the scribes, Pharisees, rabbis and lawyers of first century Judaism – that "generation of vipers"; and it wrought in them such devilishness that they eagerly carried out the will of their "father, the devil" (Matt. 23:33; John 8:44) in compassing the crucifixion of the Lord of glory. Should we not therefore regard that odious doctrine with abhorrence and fear? And should it not be a matter of anxious inquiry as to how it has arisen and spread itself among the true followers of Christ in these perilous times?

And now we come to the grand climax of the passage we are examining, Hebrews XI. It is found in verse 16, where it is announced that the fathers of Israel desired "a better country, that is an heavenly. **Wherefore God is not ashamed to be called their God;** for He hath prepared *for them* a city"; and from Revelation 21:2,3, we learn that He will dwell with them in that city forever.

Here is truth of the highest importance and most practical character. These words give us the explanation of the fact that the Eternal God, the Almighty Creator, He who is infinite in power, wisdom and holiness, condescends to call Himself "*the God of Abraham, of Isaac and of Jacob*" (Ex. 3:6, 16; Matt. 22:32).

There could be no more emphatic assertion of the oneness of God's elect, the true "seed of Abraham" (Gal. 3:7,29), and of the truly *fundamental* truth that there is just "one hope," one "common salvation" for them all, whether by nature they be Jews or Gentiles.

And there could not be a more impressive refutation of the erroneous doctrine – now current amongst certain groups of Christians – that the biblical "hope of Israel" is a thing of earthly place and dominion. This is surely "another gospel," very different indeed from the gospel God preached unto Abraham.

CHAPTER V

GOD'S WARNINGS THROUGH MOSES TO HIS EARTHLY PEOPLE

God's first covenant with Israel was very broad in scope, but was *conditional in character*; that is to say, the performance of its promises by Jehovah was dependant upon certain express conditions, which the Israelites bound themselves to fulfil. Here are the terms of that covenant, as proposed by God and agreed to by "all the people":

> "Now therefore, *if ye will obey my voice indeed and keep my covenant*" – note the condition – "then ye shall be a *peculiar treasure* unto me above all people; for all the earth is mine. And ye shall be unto me *a kingdom of priests*, and *an holy nation*" (Ex. 19:5,6).

Here are three things, which, upon the express conditions of obedience and fidelity on the part of the children of Israel, God promised to make of that people: *first*, a peculiar treasure to Himself; *second*, a kingdom of priests; *third*, a holy nation. There was *no promise of earthly territory* in that Siniatic covenant.

Thereupon Moses, in his character of mediator of that covenant, called for the elders of the people and laid before their faces all these words which the Lord commanded him. "And all the people answered together, and said, All that the Lord hath spoken we will do. And Moses returned the words of the people unto the Lord" (vv. 7,8). So the terms of the contract were agreed to by both the contracting parties.

Then God spake in their hearing the "**Words**" they were to keep, the Ten Commandments (Chap. XX); and He also gave to Moses "the judgments" whereby their dealings with one another were to be governed (Chaps. XXI – XXIII). And thereupon "Moses came and told the people all the words of the Lord, and all the judgments; and all the people answered with one voice and said, All the words which the Lord hath said we will do" (Ex. 24:3).

Accordingly the contract was reduced to writing and was executed in a most solemn manner; it being a *blood covenant*, which was the most binding sort. For Moses took "the book of the covenant," that is the scroll of parchment on which the terms of the contract were inscribed, and read in the audience of the people, and took the blood and sprinkled it on the people and said, "Behold *the blood of the covenant* which the Lord hath made with you concerning all these words" (24:6-8). Here is where we read of the blood of the old covenant; with which we should compare what is written concerning the "blood of the *new covenant*" (Matt. 26:28; Heb. 13:20).

Within the space of forty days *that covenant was broken* by the abominable idolatry of the golden calf and the shameless rites with which the people, led by Aaron, worshipped it (Chap. XXXII); and it should be noted that the terms of that covenant were *never again ratified with that people*. We shall see presently what were the terms of the *substituted covenant* that God made with the children of Israel, but we would impress upon the reader, as truth of the highest importance, that the three wondrously glorious promises of the covenant of Exodus XIX – XXIV were reserved for *another people, the true Israel*. For to them, the apostle Peter writes that God had made them apart from all conditions, "*a royal priesthood, an holy nation, a peculiar people*" (1 Pet. 2:9).

When the Israelites made and worshipped the golden calf, God was minded to destroy them and to make of Moses a great nation (Ex. 32:10). Had He done so, He would nevertheless have fulfilled the promises He made "to Abraham and his seed" (Gal. 3:16); for Moses was a direct descendant of Abraham. For the same reason it follows that, in fulfilling those promises to Jesus Christ (Gal. 3:7, 29), God has kept His covenant with Abraham in letter as well as in spirit.

But Moses interceded for the people; and God spared the people, and commanded Moses to lead them to the land He had promised to Abraham, Isaac, and to Jacob 33:1; and He made with them *another covenant* (34:10); which covenant, in respect to what was promised thereby, was very inferior to the covenant they had broken; for this substituted covenant (which was not a blood covenant) was restricted to the terms and conditions upon which God would permit them to continue in possession of the land of Canaan.

Those terms and conditions are set forth in detail in the book of Deuteronomy; where, after the recital of them, Moses writes :

"These are the words of *the covenant* which the Lord commanded Moses to make with the children of Israel *in the land of Moab, beside the covenant which He made with them in Horeb*" (Deut. 29:1).

The subsequent history of the Israelites shows that they broke this substituted covenant also; and not in one particular only, but in every particular, thereby forfeiting irretrievably all the stipulated blessings, and incurring all the curses thereof. That covenant having been finally annulled ("done away," 2 Cor. 3:11; Heb. 10:9, etc.), there remains now, of all the covenants ever made by God with a people in this world, none but "the everlasting covenant," or "new covenant," whereof Jesus Christ is the *Guarantor* ("Surety," Heb. 7:22), who fulfils all the conditions of perfect obedience, even "unto death"; and is also the *Mediator* (Heb. 9:15; 12:24); which covenant was, as we have seen, sealed with His own blood.

Therefore, as regards God's covenants with that earthly people, "Israel after the flesh," the matter stands thus: the *conditional* promises thereof were *all nullified* by their breach of covenant; whereas the *unconditional promises* were *all fulfilled* to them, to the last detail, through Moses and Joshua; and God, moreover has caused that fact to be plainly recorded, as we shall presently see.

Let us now notice briefly some of the records made by Moses concerning the covenant under which the Israelites entered into possession of the land that God had sworn to their fathers to give them:

A very comprehensive prophecy is found in Numbers 33:55,56, where God plainly says, through Moses, that in case they should fail to drive out the inhabitants of the land, as He had repeatedly commanded them to do, then as a first consequence, those that were permitted to remain should become pricks in their eyes and thorns in their sides; and "Moreover, it shall come to pass that *I shall do unto you as I thought to do unto them*"; and what He purposed as to those idolatrous nations was their national extermination and their expulsion from that land. This prophecy concerning the earthly Israel has been completely fulfilled.

Deut. 4:1. Here is a summary of the covenant. They were to hearken always to God's statutes and judgments; and, *upon that express condition*, they were to go in and possess the land. Every blessing mentioned in this book is made to depend upon that same condition. This chapter lays special emphasis upon the *Second Commandment* (vv. 15-24); for it was because of the breaking of that commandment that the Siniatic covenant had been nullified; and now God proclaims to the whole nation, and makes it a matter of record, what would certainly be the penal consequences to them if they should break this substituted covenant. And not only so, but He confirms His word with a solemn oath, saying, "I call heaven and earth to witness against you this day, that ye shall soon *utterly perish from off the land* whereunto ye go over to Jordan to possess it; ye shall *not prolong your days upon it*, but shall *utterly be destroyed*" (v. 26). Will God fulfill His word? Shall heaven and earth bear witness that He did not mean what He said?

Careful note should be taken of the promise of mercy (Verses 29,30) which should be fulfilled to them if, when scattered among the heathen (vv. 27,28), any of the should turn to the Lord:

"If *from thence* thou shalt seek the Lord thy God, thou shalt find Him, if thou seek Him with all thy heart and with all thy soul. When thou art *in tribulation and all these things are come upon thee, if thou turn to the Lord thy God and shalt be obedient unto His voice*."

This is the promise of the gospel of Christ. It is repeated in Isaiah 55:7 ("the sure mercies of David," Isa. 55:3, Ac. 13:34); and is recalled by Paul in 2 Cor. 3:16. It is the one and only hope for the natural Israelite, as for all mankind. The conditions are, "turn to the Lord" (*i.e., repent*) and be "obedient to His voice" (*obey the gospel by coming in faith to Jesus Christ*). Specially is it to be noted that this promise is to the *individual*, there being *no collective promise* for the nation as a whole. This is the mercy of the everlasting covenant which God had sworn to their fathers (v. 31). Thus it stands in the Word of God.

But compare this with the now current system of teaching, according to which God will being the Israelites in a body again after the day of gospel salvation is ended, to Palestine "in unbelief"; and will there convert the entire nation, not *by faith*, but by the *sight* of Jesus Christ standing on the Mount of Olives!

The above quoted warning and oath of God that He would, in the event of their lapse into disobedience and idolatry, *destroy them from off the land*, was never revoked or modified, that I can find; but on the contrary, it was reiterated again and again.

Deut. 6:14,15. "Ye shall not go after other gods of the people which are round about you... lest the anger of the Lord be kindled against thee, and *destroy thee from off the face of the earth*" (*or land*).

Deut. 7:1, 2, 3. Here they are forbidden to make any covenants with the Canaanites and to intermarry with them (they subsequently did both); the penalty for disobedience being stated thus: "So will the anger of the Lord be kindled against you, and destroy thee suddenly" (v. 4). For while He "keepeth covenant and mercy with them that love Him and keep His commandments," yet He "repayeth them that hate Him to their face, *to destroy them.*" (vv. 9.10).

Deut. 8:1-18. This chapter is of capital importance. In it Moses charges the children of Israel to remember all God's dealings with them in Egypt and in the wilderness, saying:

> "Otherwise it shall be, if thou do at all forget the Lord thy God, and walk after other gods and serve them, I testify against you this day that *ye shall surely perish. As the nations which the Lord destroyed before your face*, **so shall ye perish**, because ye would not be obedient unto the voice of the Lord you God."

Here God declares explicitly the completeness of their destruction as a nation. It was to be such as obliterated those nations which the Lord had destroyed before their face. Can it be supposed He did not mean this? And if He meant it, how can anyone maintain, in the face of so clear a statement, the doctrine of a national restoration for Israel?

Furthermore, the form of this tremendously impressive warning, "*Ye shall surely perish,*" is like that given to Adam, "*Thou shalt surely die.*" But in the case of Adam, God's enemy, the father of lies, raised a question concerning the divine utterance; "Yea, hath God said?" With This example and its disastrous consequences in mind, we should be suspicious as to the source of the doctrine which declares, concerning the nation of Israel, that, it shall not perish, but that, on the contrary, it is to be not only saved, but also is to be exalted to the place of supremacy among and over the nations of the world.

Deut. 11:1-9. Moses here recalls God's judgments upon Pharaoh, his land and his army; also His judgments upon Dathan and Abiram; and he admonishes the people of Israel to be warned thereby, and to keep the commandments of the Lord, "that ye may prolong your days in the land." (Over and over Moses declares that God was giving them that land solely because He had promised their fathers He would do so; and that their *continued possession* of it depended upon their obedience and fidelity).

And again in this same chapter (vv. 16,17), Moses bids them take heed that "ye turn not aside and serve other gods and worship them; and then the Lord's wrath be kindled against you... and ye perish quickly *from off the good land* which the Lord giveth you."

And at verses 26-28 we read the choice God presented to them: "Behold, *a blessing* and *a curse*! A blessing if ye obey... a curse, if ye obey not." Then how about those that obey not the gospel (2 Thess. 1:7-9)?

Then follow a number of chapters (XII-XXVI) containing "the statues and judgments," they were to obey as the condition of their remaining in possession of the land and enjoying God's favor and blessing therein; and in chapter 24: 14-26 are twelve several curses which, after they should have entered the land of Canaan, the Levites were to recite, as coming upon those who should sin against the Lord; and to each curse *all* the people were to respond, "Amen."

Then in the following chapter (XXVIII) is the solemn declaration that, if they would not hearken and obey, "all these curses shall come upon thee... *until thou be destroyed*" (vv. 15-20). And then, after the recital of a long list of the appalling evils that were to overtake them, Moses says: (vv. 47,48):

"Because thou servedst not the Lord thy God with joyfulness and with gladness of heart, for the abundance of all things; therefore shalt thou serve thine enemies which the Lord shall send against thee;... and He shall put a *yoke of iron* upon thy neck *until He have destroyed thee.*"

This was fulfilled in the Roman oppression of Israel, iron being the symbol of the Roman empire (Dan. 2:40; 7:7). And the follows (vv. 50-67) that marvelously exact and vividly descriptive prophecy, which God gave through Moses, of the final siege and destruction of Jerusalem, the horrors of which were to be unsurpassed in all history; which prophecy ends with this prediction (vv. 63-67):

"And it shall come to pass that, as the Lord rejoiced over you to do good, and to multiply you; so the Lord will rejoice over you *to destroy you, and to bring you to nought; and ye shall be plucked from off the land* whither thou goest to possess it. *And the Lord shall scatter thee among all people, from the one end of the earth unto the other...* And among these nations shalt thou find no ease, neither shall the sole of thy foot have rest," etc.

This is their condition at the present time; and it should be noted that in this same chapter Moses says concerning "all these curses" that "they shall be upon thee, for a sign and for a wonder, and upon thy seed *forever*" (v. 46).

Deut. 29:1. Here we learn that the covenant under which the Israelites were given possession of the land of Canaan was not, as appears to be commonly supposed at this present time, the covenant of Sinai (and we have already seen that the covenant said not a word about their possession of any earthly territory). For here we read: "These are the words of the covenant which the Lord commanded Moses to make with the children of Israel in the land of Moab, *beside the covenant which he made with them in Horeb.*" And this is followed by a further warning that the breach of this latter covenant would be punished by an overthrow like that of Sodom and Gomorrah; that is, an irrecoverable ruin (v. 23).

Deut. 30:1-10. "And it shall come to pass *when all these things come upon thee*" – so it was *all* to happen, and what then? Special heed should be given to this chapter, because here is where mercy is promised them; and here are stated the conditions on which they may obtain it, after they should have been destroyed as a nation, plucked from off their land, and scattered among all the nations of the earth. First there is the promise of a return from captivity if, among the nations wither the Lord should have driven them, they should "return unto the Lord thy God" (v. 2). Then follows a passage (vv. 11-14), which is quoted in part by Paul in Romans 10:6-10, and concerning which he says that "the word," there spoken by Moses, is *the word of faith which we preach,* that if thou shalt confess with thy mouth the Lord Jesus, and believe in thine heart that God hath raised Him from the dead, thou shalt be saved."

Thus we find that the *very last hope of mercy* that is held out through Moses to that "disobedient and gainsaying people," to whom God says "I have stretched out my hands all the day long," is the "one hope" of the gospel of Christ.

Verse 15-20 (of Deut. 30) are intensely solemn, and their meaning is so plain it would be like charging God with trifling (as scoffers make light of His warnings concerning hell and eternal torment) to say that this pledge, which God calls heaven and earth to witness, does not mean exactly what it says. Again we have the plain statement, "If thine heart turn away... ye shall *surely perish,* and shall not prolong your days *in the land.*"

Deut. 31:15-21. God now appears to Moses and plainly tells him that "this people *will rise up, and go a whoring after the gods of strangers,* and will *forsake Me,* and *break My Covenant.* And My anger shall be kindled against them." Therefore He commanded Moses to teach them that remarkable prophetic "song," which witnessed beforehand what they would do, and what was to befall them. "For," says God, "I know their imagination *even now,* before I have brought them into the land" (21).

To this Moses adds (vv. 27-30) that *he* knew their rebellion even while he was with them; "And *how much more,*" he asks, "after my death? For I know that after my death ye will *utterly corrupt yourselves,* and *evil* will befall you *in the latter days*" (and no subsequent recovery is hinted at; though surely, if such a thing were to be, it would appear here).

Deut. XXXII. Here is the "song" which bears so clear a testimony against them. Notice the following points:

"They have corrupted themselves; they are a perverse and crooked generation" (5): "Remember" all that the Lord did for them (7-14); "But" – how they requited Him; and then, *what He will do* because thereof: "I will hide my face from them, I will see *what their end will be*" (20). "A *fire* is kindled in Mine anger, and *shall burn unto the lowest hell*," etc., (22). Threats of vengeance are found in verses 23-26; and there is the declaration that, were it not that their adversaries would be gratified thereby, God would have made "the remembrance of them to cease from among men" (26). In verses 28-42 we find more of what was "laid up in store" for them, and *sealed up* among God's "treasures" (of wrath – see Rom. 2:5; Job 14:14; Jer. 2:22). "Their foot shall slide *in due time*" (34,35). Finally He lifts up His hand to heaven and swears a great oath of vengeance against all enemies (40-42).

Verse 21 is specially significant because of the prophetic reference therein to that new "nation" which was eventually to displace the natural Israel (see Rom. 10:9). And the last verse of all is most important in the light of the interpretation the Holy Spirit has given through the apostle Paul: "*Rejoice, O ye nations with His people*." This is a promise of the gospel to the Gentiles, to whom Paul was made the special messenger of God (Rom. 15:10). Paul had already shown (11:7) that "His people" was not the nation of Israel in its entirety, but only that part of it ("the remnant according to the election of grace") which He foreknew; with which remnant the saved from among the Gentiles were to be incorporated; thus forming the true Israel of God, represented by the "good olive tree."

Thus it has been foreseen of God, from the beginning of the earthly Israel, that the only hope of the natural Israelite at this stage of human history is to *believe in Jesus Christ and be grafted into "their own olive tree."* What better thing could be desired for them?

WHAT THE APOSTLES WERE LOOKING FOR.

It is appropriate we should take notice in this connection of the fact that the apostles of Christ, and they who follow their teaching, were (and are) looking for the very same things which were in the vision of the fathers of Israel; for as Peter – writing "to them that have obtained like precious faith with us" (the apostles of Christ) says: *"We, according to His promise, look for new heavens and a new earth wherein dwelleth righteousness"* (2 Pet. 3:13).

Thus the outlook of the true "Israel of God," that "holy nation" which is, and always was, composed only of those who are "of the faith of Abraham, who is the father *of us all"* (Rom. 4:16), was ever the same. And it was, as we should expect, a radically different outlook from that of the degenerate and apostate Jews, who looked for an age (or "dispensation" as it is now called) of earthly glory for the reconstituted Jewish nation; an age in which that nation will occupy the place of dominance over the Gentiles. Manifestly Peter could not have written the above quoted verse if he had held the now current doctrine of a millennium of earthly greatness for the Jewish nation.

Indeed the entire chapter bears strong testimony against that doctrine. The general subject of the chapter is *"the promise of His coming"* (v. 4); and its special purpose is to warn the Lord's people of what would seem to them a long delay in His second coming and to assure them that the Lord is not slack concerning His promise, as some would regard it, but that the reason for the seeming delay was because of the long suffering of God, and of His desire that not any should perish, but that all should come to repentance (vv. 3-9).

To all that give due attention to this passage it must surely be evident that what is immediately to follow this day of salvation for all men is *"the day of judgment and perdition of ungodly men"* (v. 7), "the day of the Lord" (v. 10), *"the day of God,* wherein the heavens being on fire shall be dissolved, and the elements shall melt with fervent heat" (v. 12).

Manifestly, if this present day of salvation were to be followed by a day of glory, peace and prosperity for the earth, a day in which the entire Jewish nation and other nations as well, are to be saved, there would be no long suffering and mercy in prolonging the Saviour's absence; *but just the reverse.* The apostle's reason for the delay is valid only if the return of the Lord is to usher in the day of judgment, and if it coincides with "the coming of the day of God."

The apostle reminds us that the world that existed in the time of Noah, "being overflowed with water, perished"; and goes on to say that, "the heavens and earth which are now... are kept in store" – not for a thousand years of peace and plenty, but – "reserved unto fire" (v. 7).

In verse 10 he warns us, as do other Scriptures (Mat. 24:42; 1 Thess. 5:2; Rev. 16:15), that our Lord's coming will take the world by surprise; and he couples the warning with information which shuts out all possibility of a millennial dispensation to follow His coming; for the apostle says:

"But the day of the Lord will come as a thief in the night, *in the which* the heavens shall pass away with a great noise, and the elements shall melt with fervent heat; *the earth also and the works that are therein shall be burned up.*"

And then he admonishes us as to what our "conversation" (manner of life) ought to be in view of the immanency of these exterminating judgments; and that we should be "looking for and hasting unto the coming of the day of God, wherein the heavens, being on fire, shall be dissolved, and the elements shall melt with fervent heat" (v. 12).

Manifestly it is impossible that we should be "looking for," and more so that we should be "hasting unto," the coming of that day, if a millennial age is to intervene.

This passage in Second Peter is referred to again in Chapter XV.

ERRONEOUS TEACHING CONCERNING THE SINIATIC COVENANT

Dr. Charles W. Rankin, President of the Fundamentalist College in Shanghai, China, calls attention in a recently published booklet to the grievous doctrine of the leading Dispensationalists concerning the Law of God which He gave the Israelites at Mount Sinai. Dr. Rankin cites several notes on Exodus 19:3 in the popular "Reference Bible," referred to above, which state that:

"the law was not imposed until it had been proposed and voluntarily accepted";

Also the note on Gen. 12:-

"The dispensation of Promise ended when Israel rashly accepted the law (Ex. 19:8)."

And Dr. Rankin comments as follows:

"In other words, God did not intend the Mosaic Law to be accepted by the Jews, the Jews *'rashly'* accepted it, – did something God did not want them to do. Therefore God did not intend the Mosaic Law to be a part of the Bible. He merely proposed it to the Jews, of course not desiring them to do a rash thing and accept it, and so it was the Jews who put it into the Bible by their 'rash' action. It was not even put into the Bible by human *wisdom*, as avowed Modernists teach, but was put in by man's will when acting rashly. Therefore having thus by man's 'rash' action of course improperly come into the Bible, the Mosaic Law cannot truly be a part of the Bible. Accordingly, put it out. This is the logic of the teaching of these Premillennialist leaders. And there can be no escape from this logical destruction of the Pentateuch under their teaching. To the extent of striking at the authority of the Mosaic Law, no Modernism could be worse.

"Moreover it is the most aggravated impiety and irreverence to teach that God having proposed to men a covenant, a Law, that they could act 'rashly' in giving heed to His proposition and accepting it.

"God had just led the Jews out of Egypt by the strength of His mighty arm. They were not in a position from any standpoint to make law for themselves, and moreover, the Mosaic Law was not only the necessary State law for the Jewish nation which God Himself was to govern, but it was a revelation from God of Himself, of His moral law, and of His plans for both Jew and Gentile. It contains the prophecies of the coming Messiah, the Ten Commandments, the Levitical System typifying the

Atonement of Christ. The Mosaic Code is the foundation for the entire Bible.

"And God led the Jews to Sinai to receive His Law. Under most sublime and awe-inspiring conditions was Moses called up into the mount to receive it for them. And he was commanded to teach it to them (Ex. 24:12). Moreover, it was the duty of the Jews to receive it (Deut. 4:13-14). The Mosaic Law was God's *commands*, – was His *Law*. And had the Jews failed willingly to accept it, they would simply have been in rebellion."

Beyond all question, when God offered to the children of Israel the covenant of Sinai, it was with the intention that they should accept it and faithfully observe it; and beyond all question, the law He gave them at the beginning of their history as a nation has been an unspeakable blessing to them, with incidental benefits to other nations.

CHAPTER VI
GOD'S WARNINGS THROUGH MOSES *(Continued)*

The truth of the matter concerning which we are inquiring can be ascertained with certainty by a study of God's covenants with the children of Israel (to which partial consideration has been given in the preceding chapter), and of His messages to that people from time to time, given through His servants, the prophets.

We have already seen that, by the covenant of Sinai, God offered them the highest of all blessings, but upon the express condition of obedience; the terms being, "If ye will obey My voice indeed, and keep My Covenant" (Ex. 19:5,6). To this they all agreed, saying, "All that the Lord hath spoken, we will do" (v. 8). And this pledge of obedience was twice repeated by them after the ten commandments had been spoken to them (Ex. 24:3 and 7). Nevertheless, that covenant was broken by them within forty days through the idolatry of the golden calf ("Which My covenant they brake," Jer. 31:32).

Nevertheless, in response to Moses' intercession, God continued to acknowledge them as His people, and consented to go with them into the land that had been promised by Him to their fathers. But *the covenant of Sinai was annulled*, and *a substitute covenant* was made with them at the end of their wilderness journey, when they were about to enter and occupy the land of Canaan. For we have seen that in the last chapters of Deuteronomy is the record of another covenant, which, like the first, was accompanied by the giving of the law.

The additional (or substituted) covenant was made with the next succeeding generation following that which had broken the covenant of Horeb. It is very different in its terms, particularly in that those great promises – "ye shall be a *peculiar treasure* unto Me, ...and ye shall be unto Me a *kingdom of priests*, and an *holy nation*" – are entirely omitted. (Those wonderful promises reappear in connection with God's new covenant people, the true "Israel," the "holy nation," I Pet. 2:9).

The covenant made at the end of the wilderness journey is limited to a recital of the terms and conditions upon which the children of Israel would be permitted to occupy the land of Canaan, which God had promised their fathers that He would give to their children; and as has been already stated, the children of Israel failed completely to keep the conditions of this covenant, even as they had failed to keep those of the other. Moreover, though the Lord God of their fathers sent to them repeatedly by His messengers, the prophets, to warn them, and to recall them to Himself, "because He had compassion upon His people, and on His dwelling place," yet "they mocked the messengers of God, and despised His words, and misused His prophets, until the wrath of the Lord arose against His people, till there *was no remedy*" (2 Chr. 36:15,16).

It is recorded that both Israel and Judah "kept not the commandments of the Lord their God"; wherefore "the Lord rejected *all the seed of Israel*, and afflicted them, and delivered them into the hand of spoilers, until He had cast them out of His sight" (2 Kings 17:18-20).

Nor was this national rebellion and apostasy ever repented of. For Christ declared concerning the generation of His day that they would *fill up the measure of their fathers*, and would bring upon them the wrath of God to the uttermost (Matt. 23:29-36). And this was repeated by Paul a short time before the final storm of judgment burst upon them (I Th. 2:14-16).

Close attention should be given to the last prophecy of Moses (Deut. 28-32) because of the clear light it throws upon the subject of our present inquiry. It foretells the history of the children of Israel, down to the very end thereof, showing that it would be a history of continued apostasy and rebellion, and of stubborn refusal to hear the voice of Jehovah by His servants the prophets; and it declares with marvelous exactitude and fullness of detail what the end of that nation was to be (Deut. 28:49-68). This has ever been accounted, by all who have given attention to it, one of the greatest wonders of prophecy. For example, *Keith on the Prophecies* contains an instructive comment upon this passage, from which I quote the following:

48

"The commonwealth of Israel from its establishment to its dissolution subsisted for more than fifteen hundred years. In delivering their law, Moses assumed more (much more) than the authority of a human legislator; for he asserted that he was invested with a divine commission; and he who founded their government foretold, notwithstanding the intervening of so many centuries, *the precise manner of its overthrow.*

"While they were yet wanderers in the wilderness, without a city and without a home, Moses threatened them with the destruction of their cities and the desolation of their country. Even while they were viewing for the first time the land of Palestine, and victorious and triumphant, they were about to possess it, he represented the scene of desolation that it would present to their vanquished and enslaved posterity, on their final departure from it. Ere they themselves had entered it as enemies, he describes those enemies by whom their descendants were to be subjugated and dispossessed; though they were to arise from a very distant region, and though they did not appear till after a millenary and a half of years: "The Lord shall bring a nation against thee from far, from the end of the earth, as swift as the eagle flieth; a nation of fierce countenance, which shall not regard the person of the old, nor show favor to the young' etc. (quoting Deut. 28:49-52).

"Each particular of this prophecy has met its full completion. The remote situation of the Romans, the rapidity of their march, the very emblem of their arms, their unknown language and warlike appearance, the indiscriminate cruelty they manifested toward old and young, could not have been represented in more descriptive terms. The Roman Generals, Vespasian, Adrian and Julius Severus, removed with parts of their armies from Britain to Palestine, the extreme points of the Roman world."

And this writer proceeds to show, as many other commentators have done, how, point by point, in the minutest detail, the judgments executed by the Romans in the years 66-70 of our era, were prescribed by Moses.

Now the matter of chief interest for our present purposes is that, from this national destruction by the Romans *there was to be no recovery*. And in this, the prophecy of Moses is in full accord with that of Jesus Christ, recorded in Matthew 24 and Luke 21. For Moses said: "God will rejoice over you *to destroy you*, and to bring you to nought; and ye shall be *plucked from off the land* wither thou goest to possess it. And the Lord shall scatter thee among all people, from one end of the earth even to the other" (Deut. 28:63,64). This, according to this prophecy, was to be the end of their history as a nation.

Nor is there any promise of God, by any later prophet, of recovery for the earthly nation from this final destruction and dispersion at the hands of the Romans. For an attentive reading of the prophecies concerning "Israel," "Zion," and "Jerusalem," leads to the conclusions that such as are yet to be fulfilled relate to the *heavenly* people, country, and city, to which respectively those names properly belong; and that all prophecies of recovery intended for "Israel after the flesh" (I Cor. 10:18) were completely fulfilled in and after the return from the Babylonian captivity.

THE IMPORTANCE OF A RIGHT UNDERSTANDING OF THESE PROPHECIES

Some may think it a matter a small consequence whether the prophecies of future blessing and dominion for "Israel" apply to the earthly or to the heavenly people. But not so; for the matter affects the whole subject of salvation and the hope of the gospel. It needs to be settled, and settled according to the Scriptures, in order that the gospel itself may be understood and its work properly accomplished. For so long as another hope, that is to say "another gospel" (upon which, be it noted, the only *anathema* of the New Testament is laid, Gal. 1:8,9) is presented for a section of the human race (the scattered descendants of Jacob) and that a hope of earthly character, just so long, and to that extent, will the work of the gospel itself be obscured. It was so at the beginning, when the fixed notion of a restoration of the earthly greatness of Israel made the Jewish people the implacable enemies of the gospel, and of the Christ of the gospel, Who is also the Christ of prophecy.

Therefore I am impelled to insist in the strongest way, and to call upon all friends of the gospel to do the like, that there is but *one hope, one gospel, one salvation*, even as there is but *one Saviour* for all men. Israel after the flesh was a nation under the law. As such, *i.e.*, as being under the law, promises were given them, *all those promises being expressly conditioned upon their obedience to the law*; and as such, judgments were denounced upon them as penalties for disobedience, which judgments mounted up to complete national extermination, if their disobedience should be persistent –as it was.

And now the law has been superseded by the gospel, with its "better hope." The economy of the law, with all its shadows – people, land, city, temple, priesthood, sacrifices –has been set aside, and forever. Therefore, it is needful, and is due to the glory of the gospel, and of Him Who died and rose again in order that all men might have the blessings of the gospel, that it should be clearly established and ceaselessly proclaimed that there is *one hope*, and only one hope, for all mankind. For there is no room in the purposes of God for "the hope of the Gospel" and for another hope for any. Whatever promises there were annexed to the law were all conditional; and all have now been forfeited and annulled. Its curses were what the nation earned for itself; and hence there is, in this dispensation of grace, but one way of escape from the curse of the law, and that is by accepting the mercy which God freely offers to all men through "Jesus Christ of the seed of David raised from the dead" (II Tim. 2:7).

THE KINGDOM FORETOLD BY MOSES

It is a remarkable fact that Moses foretold, in this last prophecy, that the children of Israel would *set a king over them*; and he also foretold what would be the consequences thereof (Deut. 28:36). That wicked act on their part was to be the culmination of apostasy; for it meant the repudiation of the sovereignty of Jehovah. We have His own word for this; for He said to Samuel, when commanding that

51

prophet to give them their desire, "They have not rejected thee; but they have rejected Me, *that I should not reign over them*" (I Sam. 8:7). That kingdom therefore was not "the kingdom of God," preached by John and Christ. So far from its being the kingdom of God, the truth is that *its establishment involved the setting aside of the kingdom of God.* And it was not "the kingdom of heaven," for what the people demanded was a kingdom of earthly character, "like all the nations." It is strange indeed, therefore, that any Christian expositor should regard the proclamation of Christ and His forerunner as the announcement of the restoration of that kingdom, born of apostasy and rebellion; and the more so after God had plainly spoken concerning it, saying, "I gave thee a king in Mine anger, and took him away in My wrath" (Hos. 13:11).

Moreover, this ending of that odious kingdom in precisely what Moses had foretold long before it came into existence. For his words were, "The Lord shall bring thee, and th*y king which thou shalt set over thee,* unto a nation which neither thou nor thy fathers have known" (v. 36). That, of course, was the Babylonian captivity. *The kingdom* ended then, but *not the nation.* And in agreement with this historical fact, the prophecy of Moses goes on to speak of the *subsequent* experience *of the nation,* as an experience of continued servitude to, and oppression by, other nations. It shows too that the post-captivity period was to be an era in which they should have, not peace and plenty in their land, but dearth, distress, and various other miseries and afflictions (vv. 37-48). The fact that Moses speaks of the continued existence of the nation after the Babylonian captivity affords strong reason for the belief that his prophecy gives the history of the nation down to its very end. From this alone we have warrant for the conclusion that from the national destruction wrought by the Romans there was to be no recovery.

That, of course, was not the view of the Jewish teachers, who, "because the knew not the voices of the prophets" (Ac. 13:27), and because their thoughts and desires were carnal, interpreted the promises as pertaining to a kingdom of the very same sort as their forefathers had demanded of Samuel – one "like all the nations."

CHAPTER VII

GOD'S PROMISES TO THE CHILDREN OF ISRAEL FULFILLED BY JOSHUA

The book of Joshua contains a passage (Chapter 21, verses 43-45) which throws clear light upon the question we are investigating –the future of the Jews. The passage has already been briefly noticed; but its importance demands a more extended consideration. Its value for our present purpose lies chiefly in the fact that thereby it clearly appears that nothing now remains to be fulfilled of all that God promised the fathers of Israel He would do for their natural descendants.

Joshua, whose name signifies *Saved-of-Jehovah*, had by God's express command, led the children of Israel across the river Jordan and into the land which the Lord had promised their fathers to give them. Furthermore, after a personal interview with "the Captain of the host of the Lord" (who could have been none other than the Lord Jesus Himself) he led them victoriously against their enemies, subduing one after another, until, as the record declares, "he left nothing undone of all that the Lord commanded Moses" (11:15). And finally, he divided the entire land among the twelve tribes, assigning to each tribe its inheritance, and to the Levites cities in diverse parts of the land.

God was with Joshua in a very special way; and through that chosen and well prepared instrument He completed *all* He had pledged Himself to do for the children of Israel under His *unconditional* covenants with Abraham, Isaac and Jacob; and this is plainly and most emphatically declared in the passage we are about to examine. The confusion and misunderstanding that now exist, in regard to the present status and future prospects of "Israel after the flesh," would never have arisen had due attention been given to these facts of Scripture: *first*, that God's promise to the fathers of Israel concerning the land of Canaan went no farther than He would bring their descendants into that land, would give them complete possession of it, and would subdue their enemies under them; and *second*, that their *continued possession* of that promised land would

53

depend upon their faithfulness to Him and their obedience to His commandments.

Accordingly, when the God of Abraham, Isaac, and Jacob had fulfilled to their seed, through Joshua, all He had pledged Himself to do for them, all of which He faithfully accomplished to the last detail, notwithstanding their many and great "provocations" during the forty years He suffered their manners in the wilderness, then the unconditional covenants *with the fathers* were fulfilled so completely that "there failed not ought of any good thing which the Lord had spoken to the house of Israel." Therefore, they stood thenceforth, as to their relations with God, wholly upon the *conditional* covenant He made with them through Moses, which we have considered in a previous chapter (Deut. 29:1). The details of that substituted covenant, which is strangely ignored by Bible teachers in our day, occupy the greater part of the Book of Deuteronomy. The substance of it was, as we have already seen, that, upon the express condition that the children of Israel would diligently keep the commandments of God –those commandments being of the essence of the covenant –He would plant them firmly in that land, would establish them in permanent possession of it, and would, moreover, give them to enjoy certain specified blessings therein. But if, on the other hand, they should be disobedient, should adopt the customs of the people of the land, and should forsake Him to worship their gods, then He would bring sundry curses upon them, and eventually, for persistent rebellion and apostasy on their part, would destroy them from off the land and scatter them among all the nations of the world (Deut. 28:15-68). This is stated again and again, in the clearest and strongest terms (See Deut. 29:23-28; and 30:17,18).

Certainly it is impossible to maintain, in the face of these plain Scriptures, and of what we are now about to bring to the reader's attention, that God had obligated Himself to give the land of Canaan to the natural seed of Abraham for an everlasting possession. Moreover, those who so teach overlook the fact that, if God had indeed obligated Himself by His covenants of promise, not only to bring the children of Israel into that good land, but also to establish them in it forever, then it would have been a breach of covenant on His part to pluck them from off the land and scatter them among all

54

nations of the world, as He has now done. But, as to the conclusions we should reach regarding this important matter, we are not left to an inference, however plain; for we have this clear record:

> "And the Lord gave unto Israel *all the land* which He sware to give unto their fathers; and they possessed it, and dwelt therein.

> "And the Lord gave them rest round about, according to *all* that He sware unto their fathers: and there stood not a man of all their enemies before them; the Lord delivered all their enemies into their hand.

> *"There failed not ought of any good thing which the Lord had spoken unto the house of Israel; all came to pass"* (Josh. 21:43-45).

Here is a carefully worded record, manifestly designed to arrest the attention and impress itself upon the minds of the readers of God's Word; which record declares in the most emphatic terms that God had, despite all the provocation, contumacy and rebellion of that people, fulfilled completely "all" He had promised and sworn to their fathers to do them; insomuch that of all the good things He had spoken concerning the house of Israel, "there failed not ought."

But that is not all; for Joshua, when about to die, assembled all Israel, with their elders, their heads, their judges and their officers (23:2), and after rehearsing briefly what Jehovah had done for them, he earnestly exhorted them to be "Very courageous to keep and to do all that is written in the Book of the law of Moses"; to shun the idolatries of the Canaanites, not even so much as to make mention of the names of their gods; but to cleave steadfastly to Jehovah their God, as they had done during the period of his leadership (vv. 6-8).

And then, with the utmost solemnity and impressiveness, he warned them that, if they should "in anywise go back, and cleave unto the remnant of those nations... and make marriages with them, then they were to "know *for a certainty* that the Lord" would no more drive out those enemies; but would make them the instruments of His judgment upon the apostate people, *"until ye perish from off this good land which the Lord your God hath given you"* (11-13).

And he concludes with these weighty words:

"And behold, this day I am going the way of all the earth: and ye know in all your hearts and in all your souls, that *not one thing hath failed of all the good things which the Lord your God spake concerning you; all are come to pass unto you, and not one thing hath failed thereof.*

"Therefore, it shall come to pass that, as all good things are come upon you, which the Lord your God promised you; *so shall the Lord bring upon you all evil things, until He have destroyed you from off this good land which the Lord your God hath given you.* When ye have transgressed the covenant of the Lord your God, which He commanded you, and have gone and served other gods, and bowed yourselves to them; then shall the anger of the Lord be kindled against you, *and ye shall perish quickly from off the good land which He hath given unto you*" (vv. 14-16).

It is specially to be noticed that Joshua's last message changes in character at verse 15 from an exhortation to a *prophecy*; and that, in the prophetic part of that message, he plainly declares that the then unborn generations of Israelites would transgress the covenant of the Lord, and that He would therefore destroy them from off the land. (That the prophecy had reference to future generations of Israelites appears from verse 31 of the next chapter, where it is recorded that "Israel served the Lord all the days of Joshua, and all the days of the elders that overlived Joshua, and which had known all the works of the Lord, that He had done for Israel.")

And now the whole world has been witness for nineteen centuries that God has done *just what He said He would do*. And is there to be, in time to come, a reversal of this Divine decree and judgment? Impossible. We use that strong word advisedly. For to begin with, there is no hint in the Scripture we have been considering of the reversal of this decree and of a return to the old order of things; and "God will do nothing, but He revealeth His secret unto His servants the prophets." Furthermore, the terms in which God announced through Moses and Joshua (the founders of the nation of Israel) the destruction of that nation, exclude the possibility of its restoration.

And finally, it was *necessary* that the old covenant and all that was connected with it should wax old and vanish away, in order that place might be found for the new and everlasting covenant, the "better covenant, which was established upon better promises" (Heb. 8:6-13). It was under that old covenant, which had merely "the shadow of good things to come" –the glorious and eternal things of God's everlasting kingdom –that the children of Israel took possession of the land of Canaan. And now, not only have the old covenant and all the shadows connected with it passed away, but they have been replaced by the eternal realities, which those shadows represented for that era of mingled light and darkness. But "the darkness is past and the true light now shineth" (1 J. 2:8); so there can be no going back again to the time of dimness and shadows.

It is of the highest importance that this truth be clearly grasped and firmly maintained, for it is of the very essence and substance of the gospel that, while there is mercy now for all men – pardon, life and eternal blessing – "Through the blood of *the everlasting covenant*," there is *no* mercy and *no* blessing *for any*, whether Jews or Gentiles, *under any other covenant*; but judgments and curses only. There now remains no promises for any except the "better promises" of the gospel of Christ; and for those who refuse that gospel – it matters not what their ancestry – there is nought but the abiding wrath of God, nought "but a certain fearful looking for of judgment and fiery indignation, which shall devour the adversaries." (Heb. 10:27). It is due to the glory of God and the honor of His gospel to insist upon this.

FROM THE DESERT TO THE RIVER EUPHRATES

Those who hold the doctrine of a national restoration for the Jews, and with a territorial dominion greater (so we are told) than any they occupied in their past history, usually refer to the word of the Lord to Abraham – "Unto thy seed have I given this land, *from the river of Egypt unto the great river, the river Euphrates*" (Gen 15:18), as affording support for the doctrine. The argument is – and it is regarded by those who make use thereof as quite conclusive of the matter –that this promise has never been fulfilled to the "seed" of Abraham, and hence there must needs be a restoration of national

57

Israel, if only for the purpose of the fulfillment of this particular promise.

But this argument is based upon a two-fold mistake: *first*, a mistake as to *the facts of history*, for the above promise was duly fulfilled to Abraham's natural "seed," and the Bible contains clear records of the fact, as will be shown presently; and *second*, a mistake as to *the nature of the promise*; for the promise in its fullness runs to Abraham's true "Seed" (which is Christ), as clearly explained by the apostle Paul. This also will be shown below.

1. As to the historical facts: At Mount Sinai God showed to Moses how He would proceed to put the children of Israel in possession of their promised inheritance. He would not drive out the inhabitants of the land "in one year"; but He said, "little by little I will drive them out from before thee, until thou be increased, and inherit the land." And He goes on to say that He would set the bounds of their possession *"from the desert unto the river"* (Euphrates), and would "deliver the inhabitants of the land" into their hand, and they should "drive them out" before them (Ex. 23:27-31). This shows that the fulfillment of God's promise to Abraham, insofar as it was to be fulfilled to his natural seed, was not to be postponed to a far-off dispensation, but was to be accomplished in that era of the old covenant; and so it was.

Again, when Moses had brought the Israelites to the river Jordan and was about to leave them, he reminded them of the word of Jehovah spoken at Horeb; where He commanded them to take their journey "to the land of the Canaanites, and unto Lebanon, *unto the great river, the river Euphrates"*; and said, "Behold, I have set *the land before you*; go in and possess *the land which the Lord sware unto your fathers, Abraham, Isaac and Jacob, to give unto them and to their seed after them"* (Deut. 1:6-8). From this it will be seen that, as soon as the Israelites had crossed the river Jordan, they were constructively in possession of the of the whole land of promise, from the Red sea to the Euphrates river. And once again, in this last message, Moses says: "Every place whereon the soles of your feet shall tread shall be yours; from the wilderness and Lebanon, *from the river, the river Euphrates*, even unto the uttermost sea shall your coast be" (Deut. 11:24).

Furthermore, in God's first word to Joshua after the death of Moses, He commanded him, saying: "Now therefore arise, go over this Jordan, thou and all this people, *unto the land that I do give them, even to the children of Israel*" (Josh. 1:2). And what was the extent of the territory which God gave to the children of Israel *at that time?* The next verses answer the question: "Every place that the sole of your foot shall tread upon, *that have I given unto you*, as I said unto Moses. *From the wilderness and this Lebanon even unto the great river, the river Euphrates*, all the land of the Hittites, and unto the great sea toward the going down of the sun, shall be your coast" (vv. 3-4).

Here therefore, we have a record of the fulfillment of the promise, considered as a promise of an earthly possession to an earthly people, in its widest extent.

But there are later records which make it yet more certain that nothing remains, of the promise we are considering, for fulfillment to be a re-constituted Jewish nation. Thus we read (2 Sam. 8:3) that "David smote also Hadadeger, the son of Rehob, King of Zobah, *as he went to recover his border at the river Euphrates*." This record makes evident that the eastern boundary of the territory of the nation of Israel was *the river Euphrates*." It shows, moreover, that part of that territory has been wrested from them, and was occupied by the King of Zobah, and then when David defeated the latter he did not conquer alien territory, but merely *recovered his own proper* "border at the river Euphrates." (See also 1 Chron. 13:3).

A little further on we read: "And Solomon reigned over all kingdoms, *from the river* [*i.e.,* the Euphrates] *unto the land of the Philistines, and unto the border of Egypt*... For he had dominion over *all the region on this side of the river*, from Tiphsah even to Azzah, *over all the kings on this side of the river*" (1 Ki. 4:21, 24. See also 2 Chron. 9:26).

So much for the "literal" fulfilment of God's promise to Abraham and his "seed."

2. But we learn from the New Testament that God's promise to Abraham, recorded in Genesis 15:18, was *much larger* than appears from the words in which it was spoken; and we learn also that, while

it had Abraham's natural "seed" immediately in view, its fullness was intended for his *spiritual* seed.

For in Romans 4:9-25 Paul unfolds the great truth that Abraham was, in God's sight and according to His eternal purpose, the father, not only of a natural line of posterity, but also "the father of all them that believe, though they be not circumcised." And in that connection he refers to the promise we are considering, and say: "For the promise that he should be *the heir of the world*, was not to Abraham, or *to his seed, through the law, but through the righteousness of faith*" (v. 13).

Here we get a view of the vast extent and the true character of this promise; and we see also that the heirs of the promise are, not Abraham's natural descendants, but his spiritual children. And this is confirmed by what is written in Galatians 3:7. "Know ye therefore that they which are of faith, the same are *the children of Abraham*"; and in Galatians 3:29, "And if ye be Christ's, *then are ye Abraham's seed, and* **heirs according to the promise**."

"The promise" referred to in this chapter of Galatians is the promise of Genesis 13:15 and 15:18; and verse 16 contains a very illuminating explanation thereof: "Now to Abraham and his seed were the promises made. He saith not, *and to seeds*, as of *many*; but as of *one, And to thy seed*, **which is Christ**."

Thus we find that the promise to Abraham embraced the gift of the whole world, and that the true and sole heir of that promise is Jesus Christ; though, through God's wondrous grace, those who believe in Christ are reckoned "the children of God. And if children, then heirs; heirs of God, and joint-heirs with Christ" (Rom. 8:16,17). And this makes it impossible that there should be a future fulfilment of the promise in the realm of "that which is natural" (1 Cor. 15:46).

"THE SON OF THE BONDWOMAN SHALL NOT BE HEIR"

But the Scripture does not leave the matter there. Chapter III of Galatians states the *positive* side of the truth, showing, and with all the clearness that could be asked, that Christ and His people are the true "Israel of God" (6:16), the seed of Abraham and heirs of the promises; but chapter IV presents the *negative* side of the same truth, making it evident that the natural Israel has no longer any standing before God, or any part in His future purposes. And further it is shown that the setting aside of "Israel after the flesh" is not a new revelation given to Paul, but was to be found in the O.T. records. For there is evident reproof in the words: "Tell me, ye that desire to be under the law, do ye not hear the law? For it is written, that Abraham had *two* sons, the one by a bondmaid, the other by a freewoman" (Gal. 4:21,22). Paul's question implies that those who construed the Scriptures in the sense that is now-a-days mis-called "literal," should have known better. And he goes on to show that these things "are an allegory," in which Hagar stands for the old covenant and her son, Ishmael, for the natural Israel; whereas Sarah represents the new covenant and Isaac the true Israel, the seed of Abraham, the heirs of the promise. And the climax of the lesson is found in the words of Sarah, which the apostle here declares to be *the voice of Scripture*; for, in declaring what was to be the outcome of the controversy between the natural Israel, that which "was born after the flesh," and the true Israel, that which "was born after the Spirit," and which was being persecuted by the natural Israel, he says: "Nevertheless, *what saith the Scripture?* Cast out the bondwoman and her son; for the son of the bondwoman *shall not be heir with the son of the freewoman.*" And he concludes with this comforting statement: "So then, brethren, we are not children of the bondwoman, but of the free."

It is superfluous to say that these New Testament Scriptures make certain that the national restoration of Israel after the flesh is not a part of the revealed will of God, but that the reverse is true.

THE PERIOD OF THE JUDGES

The period of the Judges is one of repeated departures by the people of Israel from the right ways of the Lord, and of repeated lapses into idolatry. Yet He exercised great patience and long forbearance with them, not casting them off for one offence, or for many; but permitting them to have one bitter experience after another at the hands of their enemies, to teach them that their welfare, and indeed their very existence as a nation, depended upon their faithfulness to Him and their obedience to His law. And again and again, during that long period of decline, He intervened for their deliverance by the hand of one and another of the Judges.

It is recorded that, in the completeness of their apostasy and the depth of their degradation, *"they sacrificed unto devils"* (Deut. 32:7). And further to show the extent of their denial of God during the era of the Judges, we quote the following testimony from their own scriptures:

> "And the children of Israel did evil again in the sight of the Lord, and served Baalim, and Ashtaroth, and the gods of Syria, and the gods of Zidon, and the gods of Moab, and the gods of the children of Ammon, and the gods of the Philistines, and *forsook the Lord and served Him not"* (Jud. 10:6).

Finally, during the regency of Samuel, the last of the Judges and the first of the line of Prophets, the wickedness of the people culminated in their demand for a king. And notwithstanding that "the thing displeased Samuel," they persisted in that demand, saying, *"Make us a king to judge us like all the nations"* (1 Sam. 8:5,6).

This was a national sin of rebellion against Jehovah. Nevertheless, He did not cast them off, but directed Samuel to let them have their own way, saying:

> "Hearken unto the voice of the people in all that they say unto thee; for they have not rejected thee, but *they have rejected Me, that I should not reign over them"* (v. 7).

This was the origin of the earthly Kingdom of Israel, over which David and his descendants reigned, and which the carnally minded Jews were, and are, expecting their long looked for Messiah to restore. And we see that, so far from being the Kingdom of God, that earthly kingdom involved the repudiation of the Kingdom of God.

Later on Samuel, by the Lord's command, gathered the people together, and after recalling what the Lord had done for them in days past, said:

"And ye have this day *rejected your God*, who Himself saved you out of all your adversities and your tribulations, and ye have said unto Him, Nay, but set a king over us" (1 Sam. 10:17-19).

Finally when Samuel was about to die, he addressed "All Israel," reminding them of their grievous sin, and saying:

"And when ye saw that Nahash the King of the children of Ammon came against you, ye said unto me, Nay, but a king shall reign over us, *when the Lord your God was your King.*"

And he went on to say:

"Now therefore stand and see this great thing, which the Lord will do before your eyes. Is it not wheat harvest today? I will call unto the Lord, and He will send thunder and rain; that ye may perceive and see that *your wickedness is great, which ye have done in the sight of the Lord, in asking you a king*" (Sam. 12:6-17).

These passages make it abundantly clear, even were there nothing else to enlighten us, that God regards that earthly kingdom with utter detestation, that He will never restore it, and that when John the Baptist preached to the Jewish people, saying, "Repent, for the kingdom of heaven is at hand," he was not announcing the setting up again of the earthly throne of David.

CHAPTER VIII
SALVATION IN ZION: THE SURE MERCIES OF DAVID

"The hope of the gospel" is for those, whether Jews by nature or Gentiles, whom God has "delivered from the power of darkness and translated into the kingdom of His dear Son" (Col. 1:12,23); for the gospel brings a glorious hope even to those who were "aliens from the commonwealth of Israel, having *no hope*" (Eph. 2:12). And briefly that hope is *the promised kingdom*, whereof God had spoken by the mouth of His holy prophets since the world began (for God had promised that gospel afore by His prophets in the holy Scriptures, Rom. 1:2); the kingdom concerning which the King Himself in that coming day will say to those on His right hand, "Come, ye blessed of My Father, inherit *the kingdom prepared for you*," whereof it is written, "Hath not God chosen the poor of this world, rich in faith, and *heirs of the kingdom which He hath promised to them that love Him*" (Jas. 2:5); the kingdom whereof it is also written, "Now this I say, brethren, that *flesh and blood cannot inherit the Kingdom of God*" (I Cor. 15:50).

These passages refer, of course, to that eternal aspect of the kingdom, for which all creation waits (Rom. 8:19-21), when the kingdom of God, into which those who are saved by grace are immediately translated (Col. 1:12), will be manifested in power and glory. It is for this our Lord taught His disciples to pray, "Thy kingdom come."

In all the above passages, and in all others, so far as I can find, where the same subject is referred to, it is always *one* hope (not two), *one* kingdom, *one* gospel, *one* salvation, that is spoken of. I deem it of much importance to establish this; and therefore the main object of the present inquiry is to ascertain whether there be any ground in the O.T. prophecies for the idea that there is *another* "hope of Israel," another kingdom of God (one of earthly character, as some teach) which will be hereafter given to the Jewish nation *en masse*, which has rejected the kingdom of God, that was preached "to the Jew first."

It is true indeed that in the O.T. Scriptures the kingdom was promised to *Israel only*, and the hope was for *Israel only*. What God said again and again, in one form of words or another, is just what He expressed by the mouth of Isaiah, "I will place salvation in Zion *for Israel* my glory" (Isa. 46:13); and it is expressly reaffirmed in the N.T. that to them (Israelites) pertain the adoption, the glory, the covenants and the promises" (Rom. 9:4,5).

But while this is *the truth* concerning the promised kingdom, it is not *all* the truth. For when Christ came, the natural Israel parted in twain. It divided itself into two parts, one of which (a small remnant) accepted Christ, and the other rejected Him. The latter part embraced the mass of the nation; whereas the former was "a very small remnant" indeed, as it is written, "He came unto His own, and His own *received Him not*. But *as many as received Him*, to them gave He power to become the sons of God" (i.e., *children* of God, and if children then *heirs*, John 1:11,12; Rom. 8:17).

Now the apostle, in the passage quoted above, declares expressly that the unbelieving part of the nation is *not* the true "*Israel*" (Rom. 9:6); and he goes on to say that "Israel *hath not obtained* that which he seeketh for, *but the election* (the believing part) *hath obtained it*" (Rom. 11:7). And furthermore, in the very same passage, he declares that this "election," which is the true "Israel," and which has obtained the promises, embraces believing Gentiles along with believing Jews (Rom. 9:24-31; 10:19, 20; 11:11-27). And now we have the *whole truth* concerning "the Israel of God," as revealed in the Scriptures.

It is hard to conceive how there could be a plainer statement of facts than has been given us in the above quoted Scriptures concerning the kingdom promised to Israel. How extraordinary then, and how subversive of the truth concerning "the hope of Israel" (for the preaching of which Paul was accused and made a prisoner by the Jews), is the teaching of those in our day who take the *unbelieving part* of the Jewish nation to be the true "Israel," and apply *to them* the blessings promised by God through His prophets! This doctrine reverses completely that of the Bible, which teaches plainly that "they are not all *Israel*, which are *of* Israel"; that "they which are of the flesh are *not* the children of God" (and hence not the heirs of

God's promises, or any of them) but that "the children of the promise are *counted for* the seed" (Rom. 9:6-8; Gal. 3:16).

Not only does this new teaching (new among the people of God, though it was the very core of the teaching of apostate Judaism) destroy the unity of the one kingdom of God, the one Israel of God, the one hope of the gospel, the one everlasting covenant, but it also deranges the whole scheme of prophecy. For it is necessitates that time and place be made in the future for another (an "earthly") kingdom and another people of God (an "earthly" people).

THE SURE MERCIES OF DAVID

In a preceding chapter (Chapter V) it was pointed out that Moses, the founder of the Jewish nation, clearly foretold its apostasy and its complete extermination; even describing the characteristics of the people (the Romans) whom God would use as the instrument of His vengeance.

The next prophet of note after Moses, who has written concerning the kingdom of God, the hope of Israel, is Israel's great King, David. His prophecies, however, are so numerous that it would not be possible within the limit of this volume to examine them. Moreover, the greater part of them are couched in language so poetical and figurative, so abounding in imagery which is obscure to us, as to require much patient investigation in order to establish the character of their fulfilment. But it is only the general purport that we need to ascertain at present; and happily that has been given to us in a single, comprehensive utterance, from the lips of the apostle Paul, spoken in a Jewish synagogue:

> "And we declare unto you glad tidings, how that *the promise* which was made unto the fathers, God hath fulfilled the same unto us their children, in that He hath *raised up Jesus again*; as it is also written in the second Psalm... And as concerning that He raised Him up from the dead... He said on this wise, *I will give unto you the sure mercies of David*" (Ac. 13:32-34).

These words plainly declare that *the promise*, which God had made to the fathers of Israel, He had fulfilled by raising up Jesus Christ from the dead; and specifically that His promises to and concerning David – among which *the kingdom was prominent* – implied and depended upon, and that it was accomplished in, the resurrection of Christ. Hence; when a servant of Christ proclaims the gospel of His resurrection, he is preaching (whether he be aware of it or not) "the sure mercies of David."

The original passage from which the apostle took the phrase, "the sure mercies of David," connects those "mercies" with the everlasting covenant; and it most unmistakably locates the fulfilment of this great promise in this present era of the gospel. I quote the prophetic passage:

> "Ho every one that thirsteth, come ye to the waters, and he that hath no money; come ye, buy and eat; yea, come, buy wine and milk, without money and without price. Wherefore do ye spend money for that which is not bread? and your labour for that which satisfieth not? hearken diligently unto Me, and eat ye that which is good, and let your soul delight itself in fatness. Incline your ear, and *come unto Me*; hear, and your soul shall live; and I will make an *everlasting covenant* with you, even *the sure mercies of David*" (Isa. 55:1-3).

Here we have "the Spirit of Christ" in the prophet (I Pet. 1:11) giving utterance beforehand to the gospel invitation, "Come ye to the waters"; "Come, buy, without money, and without price." And we have also the plain declaration of the everlasting covenant, and the sure mercies of David are one and the same thing.

As we have been at pains to show in the foregoing pages, the everlasting covenant is *the only covenant of God that now that subsists.* For the temporary covenant with the Jewish nation was but a fleeting "shadow," being likened in Scripture to the light that shined for a little while in the face of Moses, and then quickly faded away (2 Cor. 3:13-15). True the teachers and leaders of the Jews were, and still are, blinded to the fact that the covenant "is done away in Christ." But that is no wonder; for both David (Ps. 69:23) and Isaiah (6:9) foretold that they should be blinded to the passing

67

away of the old covenant Moreover, Paul points this out in Romans 11:8-10; and in 2 Corinthians 3:13-15 he explains that the veil which Moses put over his face was a prophetic sign that the Jewish nation would be blinded to the passing away of the old covenant and its promises. So that "even unto this day, when Moses is read, the veil is upon their heart."

But the wonder is that any of the present day teachers of the word of God, who are legitimate successors of Paul and Timothy, whom God had made "able ministers of the new covenant" (2 Cor. 3:6) should be likewise blinded to the truth so plainly declared, and should in consequence be driven to the exercise of their ingenuity in the devising of schemes of unfulfilled prophecy, illustrated perhaps by elaborate charts and diagrams; wherein provision is made for a reviving of the promises and other incidents of the old covenant, which the Jewish nation forfeited by its flagrant rebellion and apostasy, and which God has long ago "abolished" (2 Cor. 3:13; Heb. 8:13).

It is of the very essence of the truth of the gospel that the resurrection of Jesus Christ marks the dividing line between "that which is natural" and "that which is spiritual" (I Cor. 15:46); for the resurrection of Jesus Christ from the dead is the gospel, insomuch that if Christ be not risen, the preaching of His apostles is vain, and our faith also is vain, we are yet in our sins, those who have fallen asleep in Christ are perished, and we who hope in Him are of all men the most miserable (*id.* vv. 13-19).

Before the resurrection of Christ, God recognized as His people a nation of *men in the flesh*, the natural descendants of Abraham, Isaac and Jacob; and with them He made covenants concerning *earthly* blessings. Also He recognized an earthly Zion and an earthly Jerusalem; and He appointed an earthly temple, an earthly priesthood and earthly sacrifices. But that system in its entirety was but "*a figure for the time then present*, in which were offered both gifts and sacrifices that could not make him that did the service perfect, as pertaining to the conscience" (Heb. 9:9). Moreover, its ordinances were imposed only "*until the time of reformation*" (v. 10).

Here is a fact to which we wish to direct special attention; namely, that the whole Jewish system, *nation and all*, had a status in God's plan only *until* the fixed "time of reformation"; and the next succeeding verses (vv. 11-15) make it plain that "the time of reformation" began when Christ – not in virtue of the blood of goats and calves, but in virtue of "His own blood," – *entered in, once for all, into the true holy of holies*, as the High Priest of the good things that were to come, by a greater and more perfect tabernacle than that ordained by Moses and administered by Aaron, a tabernacle not made with men's hands, and not of this creation.

Here indeed is "dispensational truth"; for "*the time then present*" was the dispensation of the law, and it was to be (and now has been) followed by the dispensation of the gospel; for "*when the fulness of the time was come*, God sent forth His Son" (Gal. 4:4).

With the sacrificial death and the resurrection of Jesus Christ, the old system of natural things passed away *completely and forever*; and the new system of things spiritual and eternal came into being – the heavenly Zion, the Jerusalem which is above which is the mother of us all, the heavenly sanctuary, and a people – not blessed with all natural blessings in *earthly* places through Moses and Joshua, but – "blessed with all *spiritual* blessings in *heavenly* places through Christ" (Eph. 1:3).

The two systems cannot co-exist; for they are mutually exclusive of each other. That which had to do with an earthly people and earthly localities, was imposed only *until* the time of reformation. "But Christ being come" ...and having "through the eternal Spirit offered Himself without spot to God," and having assumed the office of "Mediator of *the new covenant*, that *by means of death* for the redemption of the transgressions that were under the first covenant, they which are called might receive **the promise of eternal inheritance**" (Heb. 9:11-15), the former has completely served its purpose and has been wholly abolished.

Those who attentively consider what is written for our learning in Hebrews VIII-X can hardly fail to realize the utter impossibility, in the working out of the revealed purposes of God, of a restoration of the earthly nation of Israel and the other abolished shadows of the old covenant.

CHAPTER IX

THE TRAVAIL OF ZION

We have shown by the prophecies of Moses the founder of the nation, of Joshua the vanquisher of the original possessors of the promised land, and of David the greatest of the kings of Israel and one of the greatest of its prophets, that the nation would completely apostatize, and that God would disown them and would "pluck them off the land." And we have shown that those prophecies are fully confirmed by the New Testament Scriptures.

But some will ask if later prophets, as Isaiah, Ezekiel or Zechariah, have not foretold the return of the children of Israel to Palestine, and by implication prophesied the re-constitution of the nation?

The answer is that the later prophets *could not* contradict the word of the earlier prophets – they all being the mouthpieces of Jehovah – and that, of course, they *do* not. What has misled some students of the Bible in this regard is the fact that the prophets of later times, as Isaiah and Jeremiah, predicted the captivity of the Jews *in Babylon* and their return from that captivity (Isa. 6:12, 13; 44:26-28; 45:13; Jer. 30:3, etc.). Prophecies of that class have *all been fulfilled*.

There are also prophecies concerning the "remnant of Israel" that would return *to the Lord* in the latter days. Now it is not surprising that the utterly degenerate and carnally minded Jewish teachers of the times of Christ should have interpreted prophecies of that class as foretelling the restoration of the nation and its earthly grandeur; but for Christian teachers to make that mistake is surely inexcusable, seeing that, as has been shown in Chapter II of the present volume, the Holy Spirit, by the apostle Paul, has made known that such prophecies and promises have their fulfilment in *God's new covenant people, the true "Israel of God."*

Thus, to cite another example, Isaiah prophecies concerning "the remnant of Israel, and such as are escaped of the house of Jacob," of whom he says that they shall return "*unto the mighty God.*" And he continues: "For though thy people Israel be as the sand of the sea" – for multitude – "yet a remnant of them [only] shall return." This was to be in the days when "the Lord God of hosts shall make a *consumption, even determined,* in the midst of the land" (Isa. 10:20-23).

We do not at present undertake an exposition of this prophecy, having cited it merely to remind the reader that, according to the interpretation of it given by Paul, the prophet was speaking of the few Israelites who, *in these gospel times,* should believe in Jesus Christ and "*be saved.*" For the apostle quotes the passage thus: "Esaias also crieth concerning Israel, Though the number of the Children of Israel be as the sand of the sea, a remnant shall *be saved*" (Rom. 9:27). And further on he explains that such prophecies have their fulfilment in the "remnant according to the election of grace" (Rom. 11:5).

There are also prophecies concerning those who, in future times, should "come to Zion" (Isa. 35:10; 51:11). But the New Testament Scriptures make it evident that this and similar prophecies have their fulfilment *in the heavenly realm.* Thus, the apostle Peter, writing to converted Jews (the *diasporia,* "scattered throughout Pontus," and other provinces of the Roman Empire), says "Ye also, as living stones are [being] built up a spiritual house... Wherefore also it is contained in the Scripture, Behold, I lay *in Zion* a chief corner stone," etc. (I Pet. 2:6), quoting Isaiah 28:16. And the writer of Hebrews, addressing believers in Jesus Christ, says, "For ye are not come unto the mount that might be touched" – the earthly mount Sinai; "But ye are come unto *Mount Sion,* and unto the city of the living God, the heavenly Jerusalem, and to an innumerable company of angels," etc. (Heb.12:18-24).

So far as the writer has been able to find, there is no prophecy of the later, or of the earlier prophets, which foretells the return of the Jews to Palestine and their re-possession of that land as their national home (under the Theocracy of God), subsequent to the destruction of the nation by the Romans. We have seen that there are, on the contrary, many prophecies that seem to make such an event an impossibility.

And, disregarding all Bible prophecies, it seems to the writer that recent developments in connection with the political movement known as *Zionism*, following the mandate to Great Britain of the government of the land of Palestine, and following the famous "Balfour Declaration," make it more than even unlikely that the Jews will return to Palestine in a body, or in any considerable numbers, or will ever re-possess that land as their national home.

A VOICE FROM THE TEMPLE

Let us turn now to a passage in the last chapter of Isaiah which is sometimes cited as foretelling the conversion of the Jewish nation in a day yet future, but which in my opinion, and as will be evident to the unbiased mind upon slight examination, refers to this present gospel dispensation, and indeed to one of the most conspicuous events of the early days thereof.

The passage begins with these words:

"A voice of noise from the city, a voice from the temple, a voice of the Lord that rendereth recompense to His enemies. Before she travailed, she brought forth; before her pain came she was delivered of a man child. Who hath heard such a thing? Who hath seen such things? Shall the earth be made *to bring forth in one day? or shall a nation be born at once?* for as soon as Zion travailed, she brought forth her children" (Isa. 66:6-8).

Clearly there is nothing here about any salvation for Israel in the millennium; and nothing about the conversion of *that* nation, as a nation, *at any time.* On the contrary, the subject of the passage is *the birth of another nation.* Zion is represented as *being in travail, and as bringing forth children.* There can be no room for doubt, therefore, that the "nation" whereof the prophet here speaks is that "holy nation," concerning which Peter wrote (1 Pet. 2:9); a nation composed of all who have been "born again, not of corruptible seed, but of incorruptible, by the word of God" (1:23-25).

And beyond all question the "one day" here foretold is that great day of Pentecost, which was the birthday of that marvelous "nation," the like whereof had never been in the world before.

The predicted "noise from the city" had a striking fulfilment in what is recorded (Acts 2:6) in these words: – "Now when this was noised abroad, the multitude came together." And the predicted "Voice from the temple" was fulfilled when "Peter standing up with the eleven lifted up his voice, and said unto them" – (v. 14); and when, by the miracle of tongues, they all spake in different languages, as the Spirit gave them utterance, proclaiming the wonderous truth of the resurrection of Jesus Christ from the dead. (In Chap. XII of this volume it is shown that all this occurred in the Temple at Jerusalem – See Lu. 24:53; Acts 2:1, 46; 3:11; 5:20, etc.) Then it was that a nation was "born at once."

Moreover, there is a striking significance in the words, "Before she travailed she brought forth"; for the earthly Zion's real "travail" did not come upon her until forty years later; God in His mercy, and in answer to our Lord's prayer on the cross for His murderers, having granted a reprieve for that space of time. Those distresses, which our Lord Himself foretold – that "great tribulation, such as was not since the beginning of the world" (Mat. 24:21) – were termed by Him, "the beginning of sorrows," literally birth pangs (Mat. 24:8). Hence this prophecy of our Lord strikingly confirmed and also helps interpret that of His servant, Isaiah.

The "Jerusalem" with which the prophet in this passage bids us "rejoice" (v. 10), and concerning which God says, "Behold, I will extend peace to her like a river, and the glory of the Gentiles like a flowing stream" (v. 12), is the *heavenly* Jerusalem. This appears from various indications in the context, particularly from the fact that the passage is a prophecy of the "new heavens and new earth" (65:17); in which connection God says, "And the former *shall not be remembered or come upon the heart* (marg.). But be ye glad and rejoice forever in *that which I create*: For behold, I *create Jerusalem* a rejoicing, and her people a joy. And I will rejoice in Jerusalem, and joy in My people; and the voice of weeping shall be no more heard in her, nor the voice of crying" (Isa. 65:17-19. See Rev. 21:4).

What we have said above about this new "nation" finds strong support in the word spoken by Christ to the leaders of the Jews:

"Therefore say I unto you, The Kingdom of God shall be taken from you, and given to *a nation* bringing forth the fruits thereof" (Matt. 21:43).

And He has clearly identified that "nation" by the word He spoke to His disciples, "Fear not, little flock; for it is your Father's good pleasure to *give you the kingdom*" (Luke 12:32).

Clearly then the kingdom of God was not to remain with that nation; nor was that nation itself to be converted in millennial times, or ever; but on the contrary, the kingdom was to be "taken from" them, and given to *another nation*. That Divine act of taking the kingdom from the one nation and giving it to the other (specially created to that end) was, of course, *a finality*.

And in this connection we would bring to mind that, immediately following Isaiah 53, where the sufferings, death, burial, and resurrection of our Lord are foretold, is a prophecy concerning *the barren woman who was to become a joyful mother of children*, whose Maker was to be her Husband, and of whose children it is said that they shall be all taught of the Lord, that their peace shall be great, and "their righteousness is of Me, saith the Lord" (Isa. 54). Paul applies this prophecy to the *Jerusalem which is above*, which is *the mother of us all*" (Gal. 4:26). And in the same passage he proves, by a remarkable appeal to the prophetic types, that the earthly Jerusalem and her children (answering to Hagar and Ishmael) were to be "cast out"; and that "the son of the bondwoman *shall not be heir* with the son of the free woman."

Now, according to the type, and according to all the pertinent Scriptures as well, this *casting out* of the earthly nation from all part and place in God's plan, and the disinheriting of "the son of the bondwoman," is to be forever. But the doctrine we are examining goes directly in the teeth of all this. For it reverses the order of God's revealed plan, bringing back the earthly nation again in millennial times, re-establishing all the abolished shadows of the old covenant, and making "the son of the bond woman" the sole residuary legatee, so to speak, of the forfeited promises.

ISAIAH'S PROPHECY AS A WHOLE

The occasion of God's message through this prophet and the general purport of that message, are clearly indicated by its opening words:

"I have nourished and brought up children and they have rebelled against Me... Ah sinful nation, a people laden with iniquity, a seed of evil doers, children that are corrupters! they have forsaken the Lord, they have provoked the Holy One of Israel unto anger, they are gone away backward" (Isa. 1:2-4).

Then follow words of sternest reproach, words which clearly imply that, as a nation, He has utterly repudiated them, and that He spares them only for the same reason that He would have spared even Sodom had He found so many as ten righteous persons in it. Note these words:

"Except the Lord of hosts had left unto us *a very small remnant*, we should have been as Sodom, and we should have been like unto Gomorrah.

Hear the Word of the Lord, ye rulers of Sodom; giver ear unto the law of our God, ye people of Gomorrah" (vv. 9,10).

This last verse is quoted by Paul in Romans 9:24-29, and he combines with it a quotation from Isaiah 10:21,22; from which he deduces that, though the number of the natural Israel were as the sand of the sea, yet only "*a remnant* shall be saved"; and further, from Hosea 2:23, he declares that, to this saved remnant, *God would add believing Gentiles*. For thus he applies the words: "I will call them (i.e. Gentiles) My people, which were not my people, and her beloved which was not beloved" (Hos. 2:23).

In Romans 11, Paul traces this saving work of God still further; for he there intimates a working of God's grace among natural Israelites, after the fullness of the Gentiles be come in; a divine working whereby a number of Jews will be converted and added to the one body of the saved" (Rom. 11:25-27), the "all Israel" being as the context clearly shows, the whole company of God's elect.

Returning to Isaiah's prophecy, we observe that, in the verses immediately following those quoted above, God proceeds to declare in the strongest terms His abhorrence of all their assemblies, sacrifices and ceremonies. Their oblations were "vain," their incense "an abomination," their new moons and appointed feasts "My soul hateth," He said; "They are a trouble to Me, I am weary to bear them." And this is His word to the end of the prophecy. For in the very last chapter we read:

> "He that killeth an ox is as if he slew a man; he that sacrificeth a lamb, as if he cur off a dog's neck; he that offered an oblation, as if he offered swine's blood; he that burneth incense, as if he blessed an idol" (Isa. 66:3).

It would seem impossible to maintain, in the face of these strong words of abhorrence, that God purposes, in millennial times, to re-establish once more the whole detested system – incense, oblations, ceremonies, bloody sacrifices, and all. Nothing, we think, could be more directly contrary to the revealed purposes of God, of more contrary to the declared effect of the one Sacrifice for sins, offered by Jesus Christ "once for all" (Heb. 10:1-18).

From the foregoing Scriptures, and especially from the divinely perfect illustration of the one olive tree, which represents God's "Israel" from first to last (Rom. XI), we may know with certainty His plan for bringing to Himself an elect nation, a people for His own possession, chosen from among Jews and Gentiles.

There is much more in the prophecy of Isaiah that bears directly upon the subject of "the hope of Israel," and which tends to confirm the view that there is but "one hope" for all mankind, for Jews and Gentiles alike; or in other words, that "the hope of Israel" (Ac. 28:20) and "the hope of the gospel" (Col. 1:23) are identical; there being but *one hope* for all, as there is but *one gospel* for all.

THE NEW NATION A RESURRECTION

In the Scriptures we have been considering in this chapter, the holy nation, which is the true "Israel" and heir of the promises, is viewed as coming into existence through a new birth; the national

Israel being the mother, through whose "travail" the new nation is brought forth.

The case is analogous to that of the new birth of the individual man when he is converted and become a new creature in Jesus Christ. In both cases the natural serves as the womb of the spiritual; in both cases the beginning of the existence of the new creature is accompanied by "birth pangs"; and in both cases the natural creature remains for a time after the bringing forth of the spiritual, and is in direct antagonism with it.

In another view of it, the beginning of the new Israel is *a resurrection*; and this too is analogous to the case of the saved individual, who is viewed in Scripture as one raised from the dead – a new creature in Christ Jesus, yet preserving his identity as an individual. So likewise, the true Israel is a nation of people who are "risen together with Christ"; a nation raised up out of the mortal and decaying remains, the dust and ashes of the natural Israel.

And manifestly, resurrection is like birth – a process that cannot be reversed.

CHAPTER X

THE NEW COVENANT

It has been pointed out in a previous chapter that, in God's covenants with Israel, both the covenant of Horeb (Deut. 5:2,3) and the substitute thereof made in the land of Moab (Deut. 29:1) all the promises were expressly made to depend upon conditions to be fulfilled by the Israelites, which conditions however they utterly failed to perform. From which it follows that the Jewish people inherit under *those covenants*, not blessings, but *curses only*. How immensely important therefore to them (as well as to the Gentiles) is that "new covenant," also called the "everlasting covenant," whereof God gave promise through Jeremiah! I hope that every reader of this volume will be aroused as to the vast importance of the truth concerning that new and everlasting covenant, whereof Jesus Christ is the "Surety" (Heb. 7:22), the "Mediator" (Heb. 9:15; 12:24) and the "Covenant Victim" (translated in Heb. 9:16,17 by the word "testator," which, however, has a very different meaning in modern English).

These are God's words through Jeremiah:

"Behold, the days come, saith the Lord, that I will make a *new covenant* with the house of Israel and with the house of Judah: Not according to the covenant that I made with their fathers in the day that I took them by the hand to bring them out of the land of Egypt; *which my covenant they brake*, although I was an husband unto them, saith the Lord. But this shall be the covenant that I will make with the house of Israel; After those days, saith the Lord, I will put My law in their inward parts, and write it in their hearts; and I will be their God, and they shall be My people. And... they shall all know Me, from the least of them unto the greatest of them, saith the Lord; for I will forgive their iniquity, and I will remember their sin no more" (Jer. 31:31-34).

The Epistle to the Hebrews contains (in Chapters VII-X) the Holy Spirit's comments upon this great prophecy; prominence being given to the truth that Jesus Christ is "the Surety" of this covenant, as well as "the Mediator" thereof (7:22; 8:6; 12:24); that it has been ratified "by His own blood" (9:12-24; 13:20); and that it is therefore "*a better covenant, established upon better promises*" (8:6).

Further it is revealed in those chapters that, when Christ had offered that "one sacrifice for sins forever, and sat down on the right hand of God," not only was the new covenant put into operation, but the old covenant and all its appointments – people, temple, priesthood, sacrifices, etc. – were forever abolished. Which things in fact were, even in their own era, nothing but "a *shadow* of good things to come" (10:1).

Moreover, God had never any pleasure in them, because "it is not possible that the blood of bulls and of goats should *take away sins*." And surely, as we meditate upon the contents of Hebrews IX and X, we must perceive that God would abhor the very thought of setting up again that same system of vain sacrifices and ceremonies, which He abolished at the awful cost of the sacrifice of His own Son, and which had their complete fulfillment in the "one sacrifice for sins forever" offered at Golgotha.

And besides, we have in this connection the plain statement that Christ, in coming to do His Father's will by the sacrifice of Himself, "*taketh away* the first, that He may *establish* the second" (10:9); which words, in the light of the context, plainly signify the removal *forever* of the old covenant, and the establishment forever of the new covenant. Indeed it is manifestly an impossibility that the "shadows" should remain after the corresponding *realities* have come; and it is equally impossible that there should be at any time thereafter a return to the system of shadows again.

THE NEW COVENANT PEOPLE

Who then are *the people* with whom, and for whose benefit, this new and everlasting covenant has been "established"? By the Epistle to the Hebrews it is revealed in the clearest light that the blessings of the new covenant, that is the forgiveness of sins and all other benefits of the sacrifice of Jesus Christ are bestowed upon those who are of the faith of Jesus Christ, those "that believe to the saving of the soul" (10:39); which blessed and holy company includes all those examples of saving faith mentioned in Chapter XI. These are "the heirs of salvation" (1:14). They are the "many sons" God is bringing "unto glory" (2:10). They are those whom the writer of the Epistle addresses as "holy brethren, partakers of the heavenly calling" (3:1), and concerning whom he says they are "made partakers of Christ," and "partakers of the Holy Ghost" (3:14; 6:4).

We have seen, however, that by Jeremiah God promised the new covenant to the house of Israel and the house of Judah." But there is no contradiction here, and no change in God's plans. For "Israel" and "Judah" were themselves but "shadows" of God's true *Israel* ("the Israel of God," Gal. 6:16). For God has now revealed that "He is not a Jew which is one outwardly; but he is a Jew who is one inwardly" (Rom. 2:28,29); and that *"they which are of faith"* – believing Gentiles equally with believing Jews – "the same are the children of Abraham," and heirs with Jesus Christ of the promises of God; which includes particularly the promises of the everlasting covenant (Gal. 3:7,29; 4:28,31; Rom. 4:13-16). Specially illuminating and to the point are the words of Philippians 3:3: "For *we* are *the circumcision*, who worship God in the spirit, and rejoice in Christ Jesus, and have no confidence in the flesh."

Particularly should we recall in this connection that remarkable "allegory" of Galatians 4:21-31, to which reference has been made already in these pages, and which teaches in the first place the broad lesson that even such matters as the personal and family history of one of the patriarchs were "shadows" of the spiritual *realities* of this gospel era.

Specifically that allegory teaches that Abraham is the father of the one household of faith (see also Rom. 4:16), where he is called "the father of *us all*"; that Hagar represents the old covenant of Mt. Sinai, and Ishmael the *old covenant* people (Abraham's natural seed); and that Sarah stands for *the new covenant*, and Isaac for the new covenant people, the miraculously born "children of Abraham." It further makes known (and this is the climax of the lesson) that the natural descendants of Abraham ("the son of the bondwoman") were to be *"cast out,"* and to have no part with the spiritual seed in the promises of the new covenant.

IN THAT DAY

Let us now take a brief look at the prophecy of Zechariah, Chapters XII-XIV, for the purpose mainly of inquiring as to the meaning of the following predictions:

"And they shall look on Me whom they have pierced" (12:10).
"And His feet shall stand *in that day* upon the Mount of Olives, which is before Jerusalem on the east, and the Mount of Olives shall cleave in the midst thereof toward the east and toward the west; and there shall be a very great valley; and half (*i.e.* a part) of the mountain shall remove toward the north and half (part) of it toward the south... And it shall be *in that day* that living waters shall go out from Jerusalem; half (or part) of them toward the former sea and half of them toward the hinder sea: in summer and in winter shall it be. And the Lord shall be King over all the earth: *in that day* shall there be *one* Lord and His name *one*" (14:4,7-9).

This passage has been referred to already in the previous pages, but we propose now to give it a more extended consideration.

The question that concerns us for the moment is this: Are these passages to be understood as predictions of the *national* conversion of the Jews in a coming "day," as some now teach? Or are they prophecies of *the gospel*, having their fulfilment in this present "day," which has been always held (as I understand it) until quite recent times?

In the first place, we call attention to the fact that the context makes it clear that the oft-recurring phrase, "in that day," refers to *this present day of grace*, and not to the succeeding day of judgment. Thus, the words, "Awake O sword against My Shepherd" (13:7) are certainly a prophecy of the cross. For our Lord Himself cited the words of the same verse, "Smite the shepherd and the sheep shall be scattered," as having their fulfilment on the eve of His crucifixion (Matt. 26:31). That same passage, moreover, begins with the words, "*In that day* there shall be a fountain opened to the house of David and to the inhabitants of Jerusalem for sin and uncleanness" (13:1); which surely is, as it has been always esteemed, a most precious gospel promise. It follows that "the House of David" is a symbol for the royal house, that is for Christ and those whom "He is not ashamed to call brethren" (Heb. 2:11,12); "*Whose house we are*" (Heb. 4:6); Christ being the true "David."

There is a striking correspondence here with the words of John in the Apocalypse:

"Unto Him that loved us, and washed us from our sins in His own blood, and hath made us kings and priests unto God" (Rev. 1:5,6).

For observe that here we have the *reigning house* ("kings and priests," answering to "the house of David"); and these are "washed in His own blood," which answers to the promised fountain for cleansing from sin and from uncleanness. (See also 1 Pet. 2:9). And of course "the inhabitants of Jerusalem" are those who now "are come to Mount Sion, and to the city of the living God, the *heavenly* Jerusalem" (Heb. 12:22), "the Jerusalem which is above, which is the mother of us all" (Gal. 4:26).

Observe too that in the immediate context we find the prediction, "*And they shall look upon me, whom they have pierced.*" The sense of this passage is clearer when we read "look *unto* Me," instead of "look upon Me." For the same expression occurs in Isaiah 45:22, where our A.V. renders it, "Look *unto* Me and be ye saved."

Most assuredly therefore the fulfilment of this prophecy takes place in this "day" of the gospel, and began from the day of Pentecost. For then Peter, standing up with the eleven, set forth before a great concourse of Jews, Christ crucified and risen; to whom also he addressed these memorable words: "Therefore let *all the house of Israel* know assuredly that God hath made that same Jesus *whom ye have crucified*" (compare the words, "*whom they have pierced*") "both Lord and Christ (Ac. 2:36). Thereupon some three thousand did look repentantly and believingly unto Him whom they had pierced.

Moreover they also *mourned for Him*, as the prophecy foretold. For it is recorded that "they were *pricked in their heart*, and said unto Peter and to the rest of the apostles, men and brethren, what shall we do?" That was indeed "a great mourning in Jerusalem"; for it resulted in the conversion of "about three thousand souls."

It should be observed further that, according to the prophecy, every family was to mourn *apart*, and their wives *apart*. Which signifies that "repentance unto life" and the "godly sorrow" that leads to it, were to be a *personal and individual*, and not a *national affair*, as the Jewish rabbis taught (and as some Christian teachers wrongly teach today).

Then as to the passage (quoted above) beginning, "*And His feet shall stand in that day upon the mount of Olives*," I would first point out that what goes before is evidently a prophecy of the destruction of Jerusalem by the Romans, when the city was "taken," and the other horrors recited in verse 2 were perpetrated by the Roman armies, which were made up literally of "all nations." This further tends to fix the time referred to by the phrase, "in that day." (It should be remembered also that in Bible prophecy any period of special judgment is spoken of as "the day of the Lord.")

Now this prophecy declares, by a series of figures and metaphors, after the usual prophetic manner, how the Lord would "go forth" for the deliverance of His own people in those days. "The mount of Olives" is a symbol of the nation Israel, to which He was to come (John 1:11). For in Bible prophecy a *mountain* is the common symbol of a *nation*; and the mount of Olives is a most suitable figure to represent the nation of Israel. The result of His coming to that nation was that it was *divided in twain* ("cloven in the midst"). For "there was a *division* because of Him" (John 7:43; 9:16, etc.). And that rift was truly a "very great valley" – deep and wide. "One part" of the divided nation (for the word rendered "half" means merely *one of two parts*, which may be very unequal in size) was removed (speaking figuratively) "toward the north," the region whence Israel's enemies came, and whither they were taken into captivity

83

(Jer. 1:14,15, etc.); a region that stands for the place of light and warmth and blessing – that is, the place of acceptance with God.

And lastly, the words, *"And it shall be in that day that living waters shall go forth from Jerusalem,"* etc., most certainly are being fulfilled in this day of grace and salvation. For *living water* is a familiar figure of the word of the life-imparting gospel. And upon the day of Pentecost and subsequently it went forth *from Jerusalem*, both "toward the former sea" (the nations of the east), and "toward the hinder sea" (the nations of the west); both "in winter and in summer," that is at all seasons. And moreover from that time Jesus the risen One was proclaimed as the crowned and glorified *Christ* (God's King) to whom has been given all power in heaven and earth, "the King invisible," the "One Lord," whose is the "*one Name* given under heaven among men whereby we must be saved."

From all of which the conclusion must needs be that "the hope of the gospel" is the one, the only, and the all sufficient hope for all mankind; that apart from it there is *no hope* for any, whether Jews or Gentiles; and that there will be hereafter no salvation of any sort whatever for those who "obey not the gospel of our Lord Jesus Christ."

Further references to the new covenant, and additional proof of its commanding place and importance in God's dealings with all mankind, Jews and gentiles alike, will be found in the next succeeding chapter.

CHAPTER XI

EZEKIEL'S PROPHECIES: THE DOOM OF JERUSALEM

THE BRANCH. THE SHEPHERD OF ISRAEL. THE VALLEY OF DEATH.

Certain prophecies of Ezekiel are sometimes cited as lending support to the idea of the future re-constitution and earthly dominion of the Jewish nation. But on the contrary, they contain many clear warnings of judgments to come upon the house of Israel and the city of Jerusalem; and they also contain predictions – not so clear perhaps as threatened judgments, because they are capable, like other O.T. prophecies, of being interpreted according to the desires of the carnal Jewish mind – concerning the recovery that was to be accomplished through the work of the coming Redeemer.

It must be borne in mind, while studying O.T. prophecies which relate to the future of the Jewish people, that we have a sure guide as to their interpretation in the way such prophecies are applied in the N.T., especially by Paul. And specifically, we have these guiding facts: *first*, that all the prophecies of mercy to that people that are cited in the N.T. are declared to have their fulfilment *in this present era of the Holy Spirit*. For "all the prophets from Samuel and those that follow after – have likewise [i.e. like Moses, who had been mentioned previously] foretold *of these days*" (Ac. 3:24), there being never an instance where the fulfilment is assigned to a future dispensation; and *second*, that in the N.T. all promises of future blessing for the Jews are applied *to the true Israel*, it being declared that "he is not a Jew who is one outwardly; ...but he is a Jew who is one inwardly" (Rom. 2:28,29), and that "we [Christians] are the circumcision" (Phil. 3:3).

It is very easy indeed, for it requires no searching of the Scriptures, or effort of the mind, or spiritual discernment, to say of every prophecy, concerning the Jews that it must be taken "literally," that it has not yet been fulfilled, and that it will be fulfilled to "Israel after the flesh" in a coming dispensation. Those who habitually deal with O.T. prophecies after this fashion, find the millennium a convenient, and indeed an indispensable, receptacle for all passages whose meaning does not lie on the surface. On the other hand, it generally requires both patient effort, and also real spiritual understanding, to explain a prophecy according to the intent thereof, and according to the true spiritual significance of the symbols and figures employed therein.

Keeping these facts in mind, let us now take a rapid survey of those prophecies of Ezekiel that have a bearing upon the subject of our present inquiry.

In chapter XIV God declares through the prophet the four sore judgments (the sword, the famine, the noisome beast and the pestilence) He purposed to bring upon Jerusalem, "to cut off from it man and beast" (v. 21). But some of its inhabitants were to be saved. For He goes on to say: "Yet, behold, therein shall be left *a remnant* that shall be brought forth, both sons and daughters" (v. 22).

Inasmuch as Isaiah had previously foretold the salvation of "a remnant" at the time when God's judgments should fall upon Israel and Jerusalem, and as Paul had explained that Isaiah's prophecy referred to those who were to be saved through the gospel, this part of Ezekiel's prophecy is quite clear.

In chap. XV, God foreshows the complete rejection of Jerusalem, under the figure of the branches of a vine, which, when broken off, are fit only for the fire (cf. John 15:6). There is no hint of mercy or of recovery in this chapter.

In chap. XVI, the sins of Jerusalem are denounced as worse that those of Sodom and Samaria; for God addresses Jerusalem, saying, "As I live, saith the Lord God, Sodom thy sister hath not done as thou hast done. Neither hath Samaria committed half thy sins; but thou hast multiplied thine abominations more than they all" (vv. 48-51). And then He pronounces the irremediable doom of Jerusalem, saying: "When I shall bring again their captivity, the captivity of Sodom and her daughters, and the captivity of Samaria and her daughters, then I will bring again the captivity of thy captives in the midst of them" (v. 53). And, "When thy sisters, Sodom and her daughters shall return to their former estate, and Samaria and her daughters shall return to their former estate, then thou and thy daughters shall return to your former estate."

Manifestly this is just a strong way of saying that the overthrow of Jerusalem was to be forever; since the cities of the plain, and the northern kingdom, of which Samaria was the capitol city, had been completely obliterated. God had already said to the people of Israel through Moses that their overthrow would be "like the overthrow of Sodom and Gomorrah... which the Lord overthrew in His anger and in His wrath" (Deut. 29:23). In fact, Sodom and Gomorrah are in Scripture the very type of *complete and irrecoverable overthrow* (See Isa. 1:8,9; Jer. 49:18; 50:40; Matt. 11:23). And God had said through Hosea, concerning the northern kingdom (Samaria), that He would "*cause to cease* the kingdom of the house of Israel," and would "*no more have mercy* on the house of Israel" (Hos. 1:4,6).

And now God concludes His threat of judgment upon Jerusalem by saying: "For thus saith the Lord God; *I will even deal with thee as thou hast done, which hast despised the oath in breaking the covenant*" (v. 59).

So there was to be a complete breach of the covenant, that had subsisted between God and the earthly Jerusalem. And will God ever mend or renew that broken covenant, and rehabilitate that doomed city and nation? Some of our modern Bible teachers say He will; and, strangely enough, they cite this very prophecy in support of that idea. But the prophecy itself goes on to declare, as Jeremiah had already foretold, that God would work out His purposes under a new and "*everlasting covenant*"; and that He would give to the Jerusalem of that coming day those who should be saved out of Sodom and Samaria (so to speak) "*but not by thy covenant*" (vv. 60,61).

It is easily to be seen, in the light of the New Testament Scriptures, and of the way O.T. prophecies are interpreted by Christ and Peter and Paul, that this latter part of Chap. XVI is a foretelling of the work of the gospel, which was to be proclaimed "to the Jew first," and which would have the effect of separating the true "Israel" (Rom. 9:6) from the mass of the apostate nation. The words are: "Nevertheless, I will remember My covenant with thee in the days of thy youth, and I will establish *unto thee an everlasting* covenant" (v. 60). And agreeably to this Paul declares that "as touching the election, they are *beloved for the fathers' sake*" (Rom. 11:28). Thus does God remember His covenant with that nation in the days of its youth, by preaching to them first, of all the peoples of the earth, the unspeakable blessings of the new covenant."

Chapter XVII foretells, in the form of a parable, God's coming judgments upon "the rebellious house" (v. 12); and it closes with a promise of Christ's coming as a "Branch," to be planted "in the mountain of the height of Israel." As this is clearly a promise concerning this gospel era (cf. Isa. 11:1; 2:2, Zech. 3:8,9; and like passages), it supplies us with a further indication that the prophets were always looking to "these days" (Acts 3:24) when they foresaw mercies in the future for the people of Israel.

Chapter XX contains a withering indictment of the nation of Israel for its persistent sins and rebellions, *first* in Egypt (5-9), *secondly* in the wilderness (10-27), and *thirdly* in the land of Canaan (28-32). Therefore God says, "I will purge you out from among the rebels, and them that transgress against Me" (v. 38). This chapter also closes with a view of the true Israel on God's "holy mountain, in the mountain of the height of Israel" (v. 40); which corresponds with "the heavenly places" mentioned in the Epistle to the Ephesians.

Chapters XXI, XXII, XXIII foretell further judgments that were to fall upon Jerusalem, and give details of the general corruption of priests, prophets and people; and chapter XXIV again foretells the approaching "woe to the bloody city."

Likewise the prophecy of chapter 36:21-38 is a foretelling of the present era; for the blessings of the New Covenant are distinctly foretold. The first step in the fulfilment of this prophecy was the return from Babylon (v. 24); then the preaching of Christ (v. 25, cf. John 15:3 and Heb. 10:22); then the gift of the Holy Spirit (vv. 26,27, cf. John 20:22). We have seen that His disciples are the true "Israel" and their land ("the heavenly places") is the true "Zion."

In chapter XXXVI God promises that He will gather His people out of all countries, will bring them into their own land, will sprinkle clean water upon them; will cleanse them from all their filthiness;

will put a new heart and a new spirit within them, and will put His Spirit in them (vv. 24-27). Manifestly these are promises of *gospel-blessings*, with which God has now blessed His people in heavenly places – the true Zion, "their own land." For He gives them a new heart and a new spirit; with the blood of Christ He cleanses them from all sin; and He puts His own Holy Spirit in them. We have seen that the land God gave their fathers, and which they were looking for, was "a better country, even an heavenly" (Heb. 11:16; 12:22).

THE VALLEY OF THE DRY BONES

Here the same prophecy of salvation to the true Israel, the sheep who knows their Shepherd's voice, is given in the form of an allegorical vision. The Spirit of Jehovah transports the prophet from Jerusalem and sets him down in a low lying place, a "valley" which was full of bones. "And" says the prophet, "He said unto me, Son of man, *can these bones live?*" (v. 3).

This question gives the clue to the significance of the vision. God is bringing to mind that He is the God of Abraham, *who quickens the dead* (Rom. 4:17). That valley represents the dominion of sin and death (Rom. 6), and the dry bones represent the state by nature of all the Israel of God; for we were all "dead in trespasses and sin" ere He "quickened us together with Christ" (Eph. 2:1,5). This was the condition of the whole "commonwealth of Israel" (Eph. 2:12).

By this prophecy God makes known that He would employ, in the mighty work of regeneration and recreation, the same agencies He used in the old creation – *the Word* ("*prophecy* to these bones") and *the Spirit* ("Breath"); for the salvation of all those who compose "the Israel of God," that "holy nation," is effected by *the word* of the gospel, preached with the *Holy Ghost* sent down from heaven (I Peter 1:12).

The chapter foretells the gospel era beginning with the ministry of John the Baptist (who prophesied unto the dry bones of Israel). In verse 4 mention is made of the Word and in verse 9 of the Spirit. In verse 11 is foreseen "the whole house of Israel" (the true Israel), a people quickened together with Christ, baptized into His death, and made partakers of His resurrection (See John 5:25; Eph. 1:1-4; 2:5-6).

Historically, in the fulfilment of this wonderful prophecy, "when the fulness of the time was come, God sent forth His Son" – not to set up the Davidic kingdom, for which the Jews were looking, but – "*to redeem them that were under the law*" – Jews (Gal. 4:4); and He spake unto them the word of life (prophesied unto the bones), the result being that there was a great stir among the Jews, "a shaking" of the bones; and that a company was formed; the bones coming together "bone to his bone." But there was as yet no live body (v. 7). But at Pentecost there came the mighty *Breath of God.* God began then to breath upon those who had been dead in their sins; and *they lived*, and "stood upon their feet." And the work begun that day has been going on ever since, until the company of the regenerated ones has become "an exceeding great army," an innumerable multitude (Rev. 7:9).

It is not to be wondered at that the Jewish rabbis should have interpreted this vision as a prophecy of the revival of their nation; for they were grossly carnal in their thoughts (God's thoughts were not their thoughts, Isa. 55:8), and they were, moreover, narrowly selfish and exclusive as regards their expectations of Divine blessing. And furthermore, they were ignorant of the "mystery" of the true "Israel" (Eph. 2:12,12; 3:1-6), namely, "That the Gentiles should be fellow-heirs, and of the same body, and partakers of His promise in Christ, by (means of) the gospel."

But it *is* a cause of wonderment that any of those to whom that "mystery" has been revealed, and who have learned moreover, how the O.T. prophecies are fulfilled in these days of the Holy Spirit's presence on earth, should discard what has been the accepted Christian interpretation of the prophecies for nineteen centuries, in favor of that held by those "blind leaders of the blind," whose leadership brought about the ruin of the Jewish nation.

CHAPTER XII

EZEKIEL'S TEMPLE; WATERS FLOWING FROM THE HOUSE; WHERE DID THE SPIRIT DESCEND AT PENTECOST?

Chapters 40 to 46 inclusive of the Book of Ezekiel contain the account of a vision given to that prophet, in which was shown him the pattern of a temple and its various appointments, the arrangements, gates, courts, and chambers, their dimensions and other details being stated with minuteness. The space given to the description of this temple would indicate that it is a matter of considerable importance in the eyes of God. So it will be well worth our while to seek an understanding of the vision, and to inquire as to the purpose for which it is given; and the more so because, as regards the interpretation of the vision and its purpose in God's plan, there has been much barren conjecture and much contrariety of opinion amongst those who seek to expound the Scriptures.

These visions present difficulties of interpretation, as is generally recognized; but whatever they may or may not mean, they certainly afford no support for the doctrine of a political future for the earthly Israel. Insofar as this prophecy was to have its fulfilment in the realm of the natural, it was fulfilled after the return from Babylon. But, as with the pattern of the temple showed to Moses on Mt. Sinai, so likewise here it seems we must take the Visions seen by Ezekiel on that "Very high mountain" (40:2) to be the patterns of things heavenly and Spiritual. It is simply impossible to *naturalize* (or carnalize) all the details of those visions.

Moreover, in chapter 43:9-11 it is distinctly stated that all these promises given through Ezekiel (which were proposed first to the natural Israel) were *conditional*; and we know that that people did not fulfil the conditions here laid down any more than they fulfilled those of the old covenant. Hence these later promises (along with all the others) have been forfeited irretrievably; and they find their "yea" and their "amen" in Christ, being all "unto the glory of God *by us*" – the true Israel (2 Cor. 1:20). That is to say, God will have glory through the fulfillment of those promises in and through His new covenant people.

IS IT THE PLAN OF A TEMPLE FOR THE MILLENNIUM?

One solution of the problem we are studying (a solution much favored in certain quarters) is that Ezekiel's vision relates to Millennial times; that Israel will then be reconstituted as a nation on earth and as such will re-occupy the land of Palestine; and that then the temple shown to Ezekiel will be erected on Mt. Moriah, and the system of worship described in these chapters will be instituted and carried on. This view is characteristic of that peculiar system of interpreting the Scriptures which we are examining in the present volume; for, according to the principles thereof, all difficulties in the prophetic Word, and all problems of like nature are solved by the simply expedient of postponing their fulfilment to the Millennial age. Thus the Millennium becomes the convenient and promiscuous dumping place of all portions of Scripture which offer any difficulty; and the unhappy consequence is that many prophecies which were fulfilled at the first coming of Christ, or are being fulfilled in this age of the gospel, and many Scriptures, such as the Sermon on the Mount, which apply directly to the saints of this dispensation, are wrenched out of their proper place, and are relegated to a distant future, much to the loss of the people of God and to the dislocation of the Scriptures as a whole.

The "postponement" system doubtless owes the popularity it enjoys to the circumstance that its method is both safe and easy. It is *safe* because, when a fulfilment of prophecy is relegated to the Millennium, it cannot be conclusively refuted until the time comes. All date-setting schemes owe their measure of popularity to the same fact. It is *easy* because it relieves the Bible student of the trouble of searching for the meaning and application of difficult passages.

But, coming to the special case in hand, which is illustrative of many others, we are bold to say, and undertake herein to show, that there are insurmountable objections to the view that Ezekiel's temple is for Millennial times.

To begin with, there is no proof that, even if Israel does indeed occupy the land of Canaan again as an earthly nation, they will restore the ancient system of temple-worship, either according to the plan shown to and described by Ezekiel, or according to any other plan. On the contrary, we maintain that the Scripture plainly forbid that supposition. For it was by God's own hand that the ancient system of worship was abolished and obliterated; and the obliteration thereof was for reasons so closely connected with the redeeming word of the Lord Jesus Christ, that to reestablish it again would be to dishonor to that work and its results.

Furthermore, the sacrifices of animals was a strictly *temporary* appointment, belonging to an economy which "made nothing perfect." Moreover, we have shown in a previous chapter that the entire system – temple, altar, priesthood and all – was but a "shadow" of that which was to come, "a figure for the time *then present*, in which were offered both gifts and sacrifices, that could not make him that did the service perfect as pertaining to the conscience"; that God had "no pleasure" in them; and that they were completely and forever abolished by the "One Sacrifice for sins" offered by the Lord Jesus Christ "once for all" (Heb. 7:18,19; 9:6-10; 10:1-9). For it was not by the destruction of Jerusalem and the temple by the Roman armies in A.D. 70, that the Jewish system of worship was overthrown, but by the Sacrifice of the Lamb of God on Calvary; and it follows that, so long as the merits and efficacy of that Sacrifice endure, there will be *no room in God's universe for any other*. It is most needful for us to recognize and to hold fast to the truth that the "old covenant" and everything pertaining to it – sanctuary, altar, priesthood, feasts, sabbaths, and *especially animal sacrifices* – have been completely and "forever" done away. Surely the words in which this truth is declared are plain, and the reason for it is clearly manifest. For the Spirit says expressly: "He *taketh away* the first" – the sacrifices of the law – "that He may *establish* the second" – the true spiritual worship of the heavenly sanctuary, based upon one Sacrifice of Jesus Christ (Heb. 10:8-12,18-22). And the words "taketh away," and "establish," signify something *eternally accomplished*.

THE VISION

But let us turn to the prophecy of Ezekiel with the object of learning what the record itself has to tell us of the purpose for which the vision was given.

First we would point out that, in the sixth year of Jehoiachin's captivity, that is to say, *while Solomon's temple was yet standing*, Ezekiel had a wonderful vision in which he saw the glory of the Lord departing from the house (8:1; 10:18). The vision of the *new* temple was 19 years later; for Ezekiel is careful to record that it was "the fourteenth year *after* that the city was smitten" (40:1,2). To this we will return. At present we wish only to point out that the most conspicuous features of the temple shown in this vision are the various appointments for *the slaughter of animals*, and for offering the same upon the altar, sprinkling their blood, etc. Thus we find a description of the tables, eight in number, for slaying the burnt offerings and other sacrifices, and upon which "they laid the instruments wherewith they slew the burnt offering and the sacrifice" (40:38-43). Therefore, in the clear light of the Epistle to the Hebrews and of all Scripture pertaining to the Sacrifice of Christ, it is impossible to place this temple in any dispensation subsequent to Calvary.

But an attempt has been made to avoid this objection and to make possible the locating of Ezekiel's temple in the Millennium, by saying that the sacrifice of animals in that era will be only for a "reminder" or a "memorial" of the former days. But this is a very weak effort of the imagination. For what warrant have we for supposing that God would require any memorial of those sacrifices which, even in the time when they were needed, He had no pleasure? And how preposterous is the idea that He would require the slaughter of innumerable creatures merely to revive the memory of those other defective sacrifices which could never take away sins! Surely they who advance this idea have forgotten the Scriptures which they all apply to the Millennium, and which says, "They shall not hurt nor destroy in all My holy mountain" (Isa. 11:9).

But the passage itself completely refutes this idea; for it plainly declares that the sacrifices there specified were not at all for a remembrance or a memorial, but were for the very different purposes of *sin* offerings, *trespass* offerings, *peace* offerings, etc.; also for *cleansing* the house, *making reconciliation* both for the princes of Israel and for the people, and the like. *All the five offerings of the levitical system are mentioned by name* (40:39, 42:13, 43:27; 45:17; 46:20); and provision is made for sprinkling the blood of the sin offering upon the corners of the altar, upon the posts of the house and court in order to cleanse them (43:20; 45:18,19). In a word the sacrifices are the *levitical sacrifices*, and they are expressly declared to be for the identical purposes thereof. Hence it is impossible to locate this temple, as an actual structure (apart from the spiritual signification thereof), in any other era than that of the law.

THE PURPOSE OF THE VISION

What then *was* the immediate purpose of this vision? We think this question admits of a simple answer in the light of the passage itself and that of other Scriptures.

Ezekiel prophesied during the captivity. That captivity was to be of seventy years duration, as predicted by Jeremiah. At its end the captives were to return and *re-build the city and the temple*. This new temple was to serve as the sanctuary of God until Christ should come. God's plan had always been to give to His people the exact pattern of the sanctuary they were to build for His Name. To Moses He had shown the pattern of the tabernacle, giving him at the same time the strictest injunctions to make every detail in exact accordance with that pattern. Likewise to David God had revealed the pattern of the temple which was to be built at Jerusalem, with all its appointments, vessels of service, etc. "All this," says David, "the Lord made me understand in writing by His hand upon me, even all the works of this pattern" (1 Chr. 28:11-19).

And now again a house was about to be built for the Name of the Lord in Jerusalem. Therefore, having in mind His invariable method in such case, we should expect to find at this period a revelation from heaven of the pattern to be followed in the building of that house. And just here we do find the revelation from God of the completed pattern and appointments of a temple, with directions to the prophet to show the same to the house of Israel.

Furthermore we find that even as Moses was admonished to make all things like unto the pattern shown him "in the mount," so Ezekiel was taken to "a very high mountain" where this pattern was shown him; and he was bidden to set his heart upon all that should be shown him, and to declare all he should see to the house of Israel (40:3,4; 44:5).

Again, as regards the ministers of the sanctuary, it is strictly commanded that the priests are to be Levites of the sons of Zadok (45:15); which proves that the whole system was not for an era when the priesthood of Aaron was not as yet abolished.

Furthermore, special instructions are given in this vision regarding "the prince." Now it was only after the return from Babylon that Israel was subject to a "prince," as Zerubbabel in the days of Ezra, and the Asmonaean princes at a later day.

Finally, this vision contains instructions for the re-allotment of the land, corresponding to the instructions given Moses and Joshua at the first occupation thereof. This provision embraces the whole twelve tribes of Israel. For it should be noted that in the land of their captivity Israel and Judah were commingles; and from that time onward the distinction between the ten tribes and the two no longer exists. Thus Ezekiel was sent to "the children of Israel," to "the house of Israel," and as in several passages to "*all* the house of Israel" (11:15; 20:40 &c.). Likewise Daniel confessed for "all Israel" and prayed for his "people Israel" (9:11,20); and those who returned with Ezra were "all Israel" (Ezra 2:70; 8:25; 9:1 etc.). And this continued to New Testament times, when Peter makes his proclamation at Pentecost to "all the house of Israel" (Ac. 2:36); Paul speaks to Herod Agrippa of "our twelve tribes" (Ac. 26:7); and James writes to "the twelve tribes scattered abroad" (Jam. 1:1). This effectually disposes of all speculation regarding "the lost ten tribes," and particularly of the delusion of Anglo-Israelism.

WAS THE PATTERN SHOWN EZEKIEL FOLLOWED?

So far as we are aware there is no evidence now available as to the plan of the temple built in the days of Ezra. Herod the Great had so transformed it in the days of Christ, though without interrupting the regular services and sacrifices, as to destroy all trace of the original design. That question, however, which we cannot now answer, does not affect the question of the purpose for which the pattern was revealed to Ezekiel.

It should be noted that everything in connection with the return of the people of Israel out of Babylon was purely voluntary. Only those returned to Jerusalem "whose spirit God had raised to go up to build the house of the Lord which is in Jerusalem" (Ezra 1:5). They were not taken out of Babylon as out of Egypt in a body and by strength of hand. But we know that they brought with them the holy vessels, and we know that they had, and could have followed, the pattern shown in the mount to Ezekiel. For God had commanded the prophet to show it to them, and He gave him also this charge: "Thou son of man, show the house to the house of Israel, that they may be ashamed of their iniquities; and let them measure the pattern. And *if they be ashamed of all they have done*, show them the form of the house, and the fashion thereof, and the goings out thereof and the comings in thereof and all the forms thereof, and all the ordinances thereof and all the forms thereof, and all the laws thereof; and write it in their sight, *that they may keep the whole form thereof, and all the ordinances thereof, and do them*" (43:10,11).

The blessings promised to Israel through Ezekiel were like those promised through Moses, conditional upon their faithfulness and obedience; and, since they were not obedient, the blessings were forfeited. So we are left in uncertainty as to what, if anything, resulted from this revelation to Ezekiel. But as regards *the purpose* for which it was given, we think there is no uncertainty at all.

Of course this vision, like all visions and prophecies, has a spiritual fulfilment in Christ; and this is very apparent, we think, from chapter 47.

That chapter contains the vision of the life-giving waters, which the prophet saw issuing out from the temple, a shallow stream at first, but increasing to a mighty river – "waters to swim in, a river that could not be passed over" (v. 5).

As with respect to Zechariah's prophecy concerning the "living waters" (Zech 14:8), referred to in a former chapter, so with respect to this vision of Ezekiel, we confidently submit that the fulfilment thereof is in *the living waters of the gospel*; which began, on the day of Pentecost, to flow out from the Temple at Jerusalem. Our Lord uses the expression "rivers of living water," in John 7:38; and the meaning of the expression is given in the next verse: "But this spake He *of the Spirit*, which they that believe on Him should receive." This explanation controls the passage we are considering. This will be apparent from what follows.

WHERE DID THE SPIRIT DESCEND AT PENTECOST?

For the purpose of a better understanding of the foregoing prophetic vision of Ezekiel, and because, moreover, the events of the day of Pentecost, recorded in Acts 2, are of the greatest significance, it is a matter of much interest to ascertain just where, in the city of Jerusalem, the disciples were assembled at the moment when the Holy Spirit came upon them.

Some may wonder that there should be any question as to that, seeing it seems to be generally agreed that the gathering place of the disciples was the "upper room". Indeed it is often positively asserted, as if it were a recorded fact, that the upper room was the "birthplace of the Church". But the truth is that the record affords no warrant at all for the idea that the disciples were in an upper room when the Holy Spirit came upon them, or that the upper room mentioned in Acts 1:13 was ever their assembling place during the ten days of their tarrying in Jerusalem, in obedience to the Lord's command, while waiting for "the Promise of the Father."

All that is said concerning the "upper room" is, that the apostles, after witnessing the Lord's ascension from Mount Olivet, returned to Jerusalem and went to an upper room, where Peter, James, John and the other of the eleven apostles were lodging. Acts 1:13. What appears from the record, and all that appears, is that those Galileans, during their stay in Jerusalem, had their lodgings in an "upper room". There is no suggestion at all that the sleeping quarters of those eleven men was also the meeting place of the one hundred and twenty disciples of Christ who were in Jerusalem at that time. Still less reason is there for supposing that the morning of the great Feast-day would have found them gathered in such a place.

THE TEMPLE THE PLACE

There was, in fact, but *one place* in the city of Jerusalem where devout Jews, or whatever sect, would have congregated on that morning; and there was but *one place* where the events recorded in Acts 2 could possibly have transpired. That place is *the Temple*. But it is not upon inference alone that we base our conclusion; for, after a careful examination of the inspired records, we venture to say that they contain positive proof that it was *in the Temple* that the Holy Spirit came "suddenly" upon the company of the disciples of the Lord Jesus Christ, and that *from the Temple* the proclamation of God's Good News began to go forth to all the world. And we shall seek to show that it was the outflow of the gospel – *"all the words of this life"* (Acts 5:20) – that was prefigured by the vision of "living waters" issuing from the Temple.

Surely it is befitting that so it should have been. For it is in accordance with all that has been revealed to us of the dispensational dealings of God, and of the connection between the Old Covenant and the New, that the first manifestation of the Holy Spirit's personal Presence should have been in the Temple; that the beginning of the building of the *spiritual* House should have been on the site of the *material* House. Indeed the same reasons which required that the preaching of forgiveness in the Name of the Risen Christ should be "at Jerusalem", Luke 24:47, would seem to require also that it should begin at the Temple. Into this aspect of the matter we propose to look a little later; but first we would ascertain whether the inspired record gives any definite indications as to the place where the wonderful events of Pentecost occurred.

"CONTINUALLY IN THE TEMPLE"

The first Scripture that bears on the matter is the concluding portion of Luke's Gospel whereof the book of Acts is a continuation, written by the same hand.

Luke records the Lord's commandment to His disciples to tarry in the city of Jerusalem until they should be endued with power from on high, Luke 24:49. The brief record of this verse does not state whether or not the Lord designated any particular place in Jerusalem where they were to await the promised enduement; but the further record given in verses 52,53 of *what they did in obedience to the Lord's commands*, supplies this information. For we read that "they worshipped Him and returned to Jerusalem with great joy, and were *continually in the Temple* praising and blessing God" (Luke 24:52,53).

This passage definitely declares that *the Temple was the place* where they assembled for the purpose of waiting upon God in worship and prayer; and it declares furthermore that they were there continually". Hence we need nothing further to tell us just where they were assembled whenever we read of their being gathered during that period, "in one place". We have the emphasis of the word "continually", which leaves no room for the supposition that during the ten days following, they were assembled as a company in any place other than the Temple. This passage alone seems to make it clear that the Lord had told them to wait *in the Temple* for the promised enduement.

When, moreover, we bear in mind the fact (which appears both from the Scriptures and from other contemporary records) that the Temple, with its vast corridors or "porches", was the regular gathering place of all the various parties and sects of Jews, however antagonistic the one to the other, it will be easy to realize that the Temple is just the place – both because of its hallowed associations, and also because of its many convenient meeting places – where the disciples would naturally congregate. Edersheim says that the vast Temple area was capable of containing a concourse of 210,000 people; and he mentions also that the colonnades in Solomon's Porch formed many gathering places for the various sects, schools and congregations of the people. In commenting on John 7 this trustworthy authority says that the gathering places in Solomon's Porch "had benches in them; and from the *liberty of speaking and teaching in Israel, Jesus might here address the people in the very face of His enemies.*" It was, moreover, and this is an important item of evidence, in Solomon's Porch that the concourse of Jews gathered which Peter addressed in Acts 3 (See verse 11). Hence there can be little doubt that one of the assembling places to which Edersheim refers was the "house" where the disciples were "sitting" when the Holy Spirit came upon them.

When Luke takes up, in the book of Acts, the thread of the narrative he dropped at the end of his Gospel, he says (speaking of the apostles) that "These all *continued* (lit. were continuing) with *one accord* in prayer and supplication with the women, and Mary the mother of Jesus, and with His brethren." (Acts 1:14). We have here in substance a repetition of what is recorded in the last verse of Luke's Gospel, namely that, during the ten days following the Lord's ascension, His disciples were "continually" together waiting upon God (they "continued with one accord in prayer and supplication"). The record in Acts omits mention of the place where they so continued' but that information was not needed, seeing it had already been definitely stated in Luke 24:52,53. But the evangelist adds the interesting facts that the women, Mary the mother of the Lord, and His brethren, were with them. All this, be it remembered, was done by the Lord's express instructions. They were of course praying for the promised enduement from on high (Luke 11:13).

The next verse (Acts 1:15), states that "in those days (of waiting upon God in the Temple) Peter stood up in the midst of the disciples and said (the number of names together were about an hundred and twenty)", – and then follows the account of the choosing of Matthias as an apostle and witness of Christ's resurrection in the place of Judas. This *doubtless* occurred in their *accustomed gathering place* in the Temple, since they were "continually" there during those days of waiting for enduement form on high.

In passing we would note how unlikely it is that the disciples, to the number of one hundred and twenty, should (or could) be using their place of gathering the "upper room" which served the apostles for sleeping quarters.

THE DAY OF PENTECOST

Thus the day of Pentecost came; and the occurrence of the *great Feast-day* would furnish an *additional reason* why they should be found assembled in the Temple. The services – the offering of the morning sacrifice and incense, with the accompanying prayers (in which they would undoubtedly have taken part) – began at sunrise. This service being concluded, they would naturally be "sitting" in their customary place; and then it was that "suddenly" out of heaven came that sound "as of a rushing wind." The words "they were *all* with *one accord* in one place" (compare 1:14) indicate that they were in their customary gathering place in the Temple. Similar words found at the end of chapter 2 lend emphasis to this; for we find there the statement that, after about three thousand souls had been "added" to them, they still continued *with one accord in the Temple* (Verse 46). This shows that what they had been doing as a small company they "continued" to do, still "with one accord," as an exceedingly large and *growing* company. It shows further that the place where they were gathered when the Holy Spirit came upon them must have been of such dimensions as to admit of *three thousand more being "added" to them*; and it need hardly be said that the Temple was the *only building in Jerusalem open to the public*, where this would have been possible.

By having before our eye the several statements of Scripture that bear upon the matter we are examining it will be seen, we think, that there is no room for doubt about it. These are the statements:

Luke 24:52,53. "And they worshipped Him, and returned to Jerusalem with great joy, and were *continually* in the Temple, praising and blessing God."

Acts 1:14. "All these were *continuing* with one accord in prayer and supplication, with the women, and Mary the mother of Jesus, and with His brethren."

This must needs have been in the Temple, since it is impossible that they should have been "*continually* in the Temple" and at the same time should have been "continuing with one accord" in another place.

Acts 2:1. "And when the day of Pentecost was fully come, they were all *with one accord in one place.*"

Acts 2:46. "And they, *continuing daily with one accord in the Temple.*"

These passages reiterate that the disciple *continued*, during all the period in question, in *one place*; and the first and last passages quoted state that the place was the Temple.

From the last passage it plainly appears that, after Pentecost, they still made it a practice to meet "daily in the Temple", the wording being such as to show that this was not a new custom from that date, but was the "continuing" of what had been their custom since the Lord's ascension into heaven.

THE SERVICE OF THE FEAST OF PENTECOST

Additional light upon our subject is afforded by Acts 2:1, when heed is given to the literal meaning of that verse. As rendered in our *Authorized* Version it reads "And when the day of *Pentecost was fully come.*" The word translated by the three English words "*was fully come*" (which rendering manifestly does not give the true sense, since a day cannot be more "fully come" after it has actually come), means literally "*was being accomplished.*" In Bagster interlinear translation the reading is: "And *during the accomplishing* of the day of Pentecost, they were all with one accord in *the same* place."

What is seemingly implied is that they were, as we should expect, in the Temple, for the purpose of taking part in the appointed services of the great feast day. During an intermission in those ceremonies they would naturally be "sitting" together in their customary meeting-place within the Temple area. What seems to be impressed upon us by this verse is that, during the accomplishing of the various ceremonies of the day of Pentecost, the disciples were not dispersed and mingled with the great crowds of worshippers, but *kept together*, and were with one accord in one place – not scattered about. It can hardly be doubted, therefore, that at the moment the Spirit descended upon them they were all in one and the place somewhere within the large area of the Temple, presumably in Solomon's Porch.

Concerning the verse we are now considering (Acts 2:1), Dr. G. Campbell Morgan, in a letter to the author, said: "Personally, I believe that the statement that the day of Pentecost '*was being fulfilled*' means far more than that they were observing its ritual. I am convinced that the meaning of Luke here is that *all that was signified by that feast was finding its historic fulfilment.*"

With the aid of this comment we can see a great wealth of meaning in these few words of Scripture.

The coming of the Holy Spirit took place some little time before nine in the morning (see verse 15), just long enough for it to be "noised abroad" (2:6), and for an enormous crowd to congregate. There would be ample time for this between the morning services and nine o'clock.

On reading attentively the record of verses 1-14 it will be seen that the events there narrated happened *all in one and the same locality*; for there is no change of location. Wherever the disciples were when they began to speak in other (*heteros*-different) tongues or languages, and where the astonished multitude assembled and listened to the first Gospel address ever preached "with the Holy Ghost come down from heaven," that was the very same place where the Holy Spirit came upon them.

Concerning the words of verse 6, "Now when this was noised abroad," Dr. Morgan, in the letter already quoted, says that this is not to be taken as meaning that a rumor of the marvelous event was spread abroad; for the verb rendered "noised broad" in the A.V. "is never used in the sense of a rumor. I believe *the sound as of a mighty wind was heard by the entire city.* That being so, your interpretation as to the place falls in with tremendous naturalness to me. The devout Jews would, at the hearing of some supernatural sound, *rush to the Temple.*" In this connection the force of the words of Acts 2:2 should be specially noted: "*And suddenly there came a sound from heaven as of a rushing mighty wind (or Breath) and it filled all the house* where they *were sitting*."

It is important to note that in those days, and for a considerable period thereafter, the disciples were in "favor with all the people" (Acts 2:48); and hence they were permitted to enjoy, in common with all Jewish sects and parties, the privileges of assembling for the usual purposes, and as a distinct company or sect, in the Temple. It should also be specially noted that no pious Jews would be anywhere but in the Temple on that day. (See Acts 20:16).

We conclude, therefore, that the *material* House of God served as the womb for the *spiritual* House, and that from it the Church was to come forth, and soon did come forth. For a little while the two were identified, as the true spiritual "Israel of God" was, for awhile, identified with "Israel after the flesh" – the spiritual seed of Abraham with his natural seed. And this is in keeping with the revealed ways of God.

The letter from Dr. Morgan, from which several quotations have been given above, was written in reply to one from the author, in which he submitted this interpretation of Acts II, and asked Dr. Morgan's opinion thereon. Dr. Morgan stated in reply that the interpretation was new to him; and he went on to say:

"I have not the slightest hesitation in saying that you are absolutely correct. Here is an illustration of those of us who desire and attempt to be the most careful in our study, are in danger of taking things too much for granted. I certainly have proceeded on the assumption that the 'one place' of Acts II was the 'upper room' of Acts I. It is as plain as a thing can be that I have been wrong; and I am very grateful to have it thus pointed out."

THE SOURCE OF THE LIVING WATERS

It is evident that the matter into which we have been inquiring has a direct relation to certain prophecies, such as Ezekiel 47, referred to above, where the prophet describes his vision of the healing and life-giving waters issuing from *out of the Temple*. IT was explained to the prophet, as we have already noted, that the water which he saw were to go down into the desert (which suggests barren Israel), and to go into the sea (which symbolizes the nations), whose waters should be healed; and the description continues, –

> "And it shall come to pass that everything that liveth which moveth, withersoever the rivers shall come, shall live; and there shall be a very great multitude of fish, because these waters shall come thither; for they shall be healed. And everything shall live wither the river cometh" (Ezek. 47:9).

It is easy to see in this passage the familiar scriptural figures of the Gospel, and its life-giving and healing ministry. So we note with interest that the Temple – the House of God – was to be the source of the stream of living waters.

Therefore, we cannot fail to see in this prophetic vision a spiritual foretelling of the issuing forth of the Gospel for all mankind from God's appointed center, which broadly was Israel, and more definitely Jerusalem, and still more definitely the Temple. Other portions of Ezekiel's prophecy have clearly a spiritual fulfilment in this dispensation of the Holy Spirit, as we have sought to show.

In this connection we would call attention also to the prophecy of Joel. Inasmuch as the Apostle Peter quoted from the second chapter of Joel, as having its fulfilment in the coming of the Holy Spirit, and in those miraculous events whereby His presence was manifested, it is significant that, in chapter 3, of Joel's prophecy, there is the promise that "all of the rivers of Judah will flow with waters, and a fountain shall come forth of the *House of the Lord*". (3:18). We believe that those who are spiritual will be able to see in this verse and its context much that is applicable to this present dispensation, though it may be that the complete fulfilment of this passage, and also of that quoted by Peter from chapter 2, awaits the coming again of the Lord from heaven.

"GO SPEAK IN THE TEMPLE ALL THE WORDS OF THIS LIFE"

Further, we have the very significant record of Acts 5:17-25, which tells us that when the Apostles were released by the angel of the Lord from the prison into which the religious leaders had put them, the angel bade them, "Go, stand and speak *in the Temple*, to the people all *the words of this life*." (v. 20). This makes clear, for reasons which we should seek to discern, that it was in the purpose of God that the gospel-stream – "the words of this life" – should begin their flow in the Temple. In this we can see the continuity of God's dealings and the orderly working out of His great plan. Everything pertaining to the old dispensation centered in the Temple. Therefore, it was fitting that the new dispensation should start at that place, and move out thence into the world which it was to overspread.

The phrase "words of *this life*" is very significant; and it is moreover, an aid to the right understanding of the passage; for it serves to elucidate the meaning of the expression "living waters" in the prophecies.

And, finally, the Scripture tells us that, notwithstanding the strong opposition of the authorities, the disciples ceased not daily, *in the temple*, and in every house, to teach and preach Jesus Christ. (Acts 5:40-42).

LIVING WATERS FLOWING FROM THE HOUSE OF GOD

For some time after Pentecost the church continued at Jerusalem, and seems to have been tolerated, in accordance with the advice of Gamaliel (Acts 5:33-40) until the time of the stoning of Stephen, after which period the gospel stream spread throughout Judea and Samaria (Acts 8:1), the church at Jerusalem, the spiritual house of God, being thus far its source. A little later we find another "church" of God at Antioch; for it is written that Barnabas sought Saul at Tarsus, and brought him unto Antioch, and that for "a whole year they assembled themselves *with the church*, and taught much people" (Acts 11:25,26). Here again in "the church" in Antioch we find the Holy Spirit in full charge; and after a year of teaching *inside* the House, we see the living waters *flowing out*, and producing the results intended in the purposes of God. For we read at Acts 13:1,2, concerning "the church that was at Antioch", that "as they ministered to the Lord and fasted, the Holy Ghost said, Separate Me Barnabas and Saul for the work thereunto I have called them." And thus, from the House of God, and in the power of the Spirit of God, the stream of the Gospel flowed out in a new direction, and extended farther than it had yet gone.

Still later on the gospel was carried into Europe and it came to Thessalonica – not in word only, but also in power, *and in the Holy Ghost*, and in much assurance (1 Thess. 1:5). The result was "the church of the Thessalonians in God the Father, and in the Lord Jesus Christ" (1:1). And this is declared to be an "example" or pattern for other churches, for the express reason, as the apostle writes to them that, "From you *sounded out the Word of the Lord*, not only in Macedonia and Achaia, but also in every place your faith to God-ward is spread abroad." (1:8).

A GREAT DIFFERENCE

Our study brings into view a great difference between the Temple – God's dwelling place in the old dispensation, and the Church – His dwelling place in the new. In the case of the Temple, sacrifices were brought *to* it, blood flowed in it, and incense (worship) ascended *from* it. But *no healing waters flowed from it.* Hence what Ezekiel saw, and what was revealed also to Joel and to Zechariah, living waters going out from Jerusalem (Joel 3:18; Zech. 14:8), was *something quite new*, and to which the Temple and its ritual presented no analogy.

Therefore, one of the chief lessons to be learned from the Scriptures we have been considering is that the "Spiritual House" of this era should be specially marked by being the source of a freely flowing stream of living waters, carrying life and health into all the regions round about. And where this mark is lacking, even when the form of the House is quite correct, the explanation will doubtless be found in the conditions *inside the House*.

CHAPTER XIII

WHAT THE N.T. TEACHES AS TO FUTURE MERCY FOR THE JEWS

Before turning to the New Testament for the purpose of considering certain passages that throw light upon the subject, we would remind the reader of the need of giving particular attention to what is written on that subject in the N.T. Scriptures. Chief among the reasons for this need is the fact that the prophecies of the Old Testament are occupied principally with the coming of the Messiah, the promised and long expected Son of David, for the redemption of His people, "as He spake by the mouth of His holy prophets, which have been since the world began" (Lu. 1:70). Those prophecies did not, except in a few instances, look beyond the events of this present era of the Holy Spirit.

In accordance with what had been predicted by the prophets of Israel, "when the fullness of the time was come" – for the fulfilment of their prophecies – "God sent forth His Son ... *to redeem* them that were under the law" (Gal. 4:4,5). But they had been taught by their "blind leaders" to look for a physical and political redemption, instead of a spiritual redemption from the dominion of sin and death, which was what their prophets had foretold. Consequently when the Divine Redeemer "came to His own [creation] His own [people] received Him not" (John 1:11); but rejected Him, betrayed Him, and compassed His death.

Needless to say, this unparalleled crime brought about an entirely different situation from that which had previously existed respecting the relationship between God and that people. Not that God was taken by surprise, and therefore constrained to re-shape His plans; for all had been foreseen; and all that happened was in strict accordance with the determinate counsel and foreknowledge of God, and for the furtherance of the eternal purpose, which He had purposed in Christ Jesus our Lord.

As to this there is no disagreement amongst those who hold the fundamentals of the Christian faith; and I think it is also generally agreed that, with the first coming of Christ, and with His death, resurrection and ascension, and the coming of the Holy Spirit, the era began which had been foretold by the prophets, the era when God would have another "people"; when He would say to them which were not His people, "Thou art My people"; and they should say, "Thou art my God" (Hos. 2:23). Indeed, the apostle Paul cites this very prophecy of Hosea and expounds it as referring to the people God is *now* calling to Himself out of all nations through the gospel; not from out "of the Jews only, but also of the Gentiles" (Rom. 9:24-26). And this quotation is from the passage in which Paul explains who the true "Israel" is, to whom the promises were made; and in which, after stating, in the plainest of words that "They are not all *Israel* which are of Israel" (v. 9), he shows that, in fact, but a few – "a remnant" (v. 27) – of the naturally born Israelites, were embraced in the true "Israel," and that the full number of the people of God was to be made up of the saved from among the Gentiles. This is what Hosea and other prophets had foretold, though God purposely enveloped the meaning of their prophecies and His full purposes for the Gentiles, in "mystery," which mystery is now fully explained (Eph. 3:1-6).

Evidently then, as regards the purposes of God concerning the Jewish people after their rejection of that One through whom their promised redemption was to come, *we must needs look to what is revealed in the New Testament*; for there is where the Spirit of God has revealed "the fellowship of the mystery" (Eph. 3:9), that is, the union of Jews and Gentiles to form the true Israel.

Let us recall, moreover, that the covenant relations between God and "Israel after the flesh" were ended, even as had been foretold by their own prophets, beginning with Moses and Joshua (Deut. 4:26; 6:14, 15; 8:20; Josh. 23:15,16); the old covenant was dissolved and "ready to vanish away"; every vestige of it was shortly to be obliterated; and therefore, of necessity, all promises based upon that covenant, had there been any as yet unfulfilled, fell to the ground. But beside all that, God has now brought clearly to light, as we have seen, what He had but dimly revealed in times past, that the name ISRAEL belongs properly to His new-covenant people.

Therefore, it is not enough, for the settling of the question of God's future purposes for the Jews, that prophecies concerning Israel be found which apparently have not yet been fulfilled; for we must needs conclude, as to all such prophecies – unless the contrary plainly appears – that they pertain to the true "Israel of God," and that their fulfillment is in the realm of things spiritual and unseen.

What then does the New Testament say as to the reconstitution hereafter of the Jewish nation; as to the re-occupation by that nation of the land of Canaan; as to its exaltation to the place of world-supremacy and headship over other nations; as to the re-building of the temple and the re-constitution of bloody sacrifices &c.? *Not one word.*

This silence is itself sufficient to dispose of the question before us; but there is much more than that to be learned from the New Testament; for there are statements in it which make it *utterly impossible* that there should be any such future in store for the Jewish nation. Some of those New Testament statements have been quoted in the preceding portion of this volume, and other will be cited hereafter.

Again it is particularly to be observed that, in "the manifold wisdom of God," and because of His foreknowledge of the rejection of the Messiah by His nominal people, He saw fit to conceal for a time, in the form of "mystery" (Eph. 3:1-12 and "allegory" (Gal. 4:22-26), the fact that the things historical and prophetic pertaining to "Israel after the flesh" were but the temporal foreshadowings (Heb. 10:1) of things eternal and spiritual; which mystery therefore "in other ages was not made known unto the sons of men, as it is now revealed unto His holy apostles and prophets by the Spirit" (Eph. 3:5).

That "mystery" (which is not a *mystery* any longer) comprised several elements, whereof the most prominent (and the hardest for the Jewish mind to grasp) *was the place which believing Gentiles were to have in "the commonwealth of Israel,"* and the share that was to be theirs in "the covenants of promise" (Eph. 2:12); that Gentiles were in the eternal purpose of God, destined to be *"joint-heirs"* (with natural Israelites), *"and a joint-body, and joint-partakers of His promise in Christ, by means of the gospel"* (literal

111

rendering of Eph. 3:6). And what is particularly pertinent to our present inquiry is the previously hidden, "but *now* clearly revealed, fact, that the true "Israel of God" (Gal. 6:16), the true "seed of Abraham" who are the heirs of all the promises of God (Gal. 3:7, 29; 2 Cor. 1:20) are a body composed of all those – whether by nature they are Jews or Gentiles – who are "of the *faith* of Abraham; who is the father of us *all*" (Rom. 4:16).

Because of this "mystery of Christ" (Eph. 3:4) which Paul was specially commissioned to explain, it is most needful that we, in attempting the interpretation of the O.T. prophecies concerning Israel, Zion, Jerusalem, etc., should take pains to ascertain whether it was the earthly and natural people (or locality) the prophet had in view, or the heavenly and spiritual counterpart thereof. Happily it is generally possible, in the light of the explanations given in the New Testament, to do this with some degree of certainty.

Moreover, it will be found that, when we have set aside *first,* all the O.T. prophecies and promises concerning Israel that have been already fulfilled, *second,* all that were conditional in character and hence have become null and void for failure by the Jews to perform the conditions on which they were based, and *third,* those that belong to "the Israel of God," there remains for the natural Israel no promises of blessing except "the common salvation" (Jude 3) which is proclaimed by the gospel of Christ, and which God bestows freely upon all – Jews and Gentiles – who fulfill the conditions of "repentance toward God and faith toward our Lord Jesus Christ" (Acts 20:21).

Further, before taking up the passages of the New Testament that are relevant to our subject, we would recall to the reader's mind what is said in chapter II of this volume regarding what is commonly called the "literal" interpretation of the prophecies.

What we specially wish the reader to understand is that the *literal* interpretation of a prophecy may require it to be understood in the *spiritual* sense. For, as regards Israel, Zion, Jerusalem, the Land of Promise, &c. the spiritual and heavenly thing so designated is the *real* thing and is often (as the N.T. abundantly proves) what was *literally* intended. In Scripture the contrast is not between the *literal* and the spiritual, but between the *natural* and the spiritual; as it is

112

written: "Howbeit that was not first which is *spiritual*, but that which is *natural*; and afterward that which is spiritual. The first man is of *the earth*, earthly; the second man is from the Lord from *heaven*" (1 Cor. 15:46,47). These words reveal the rule or principle of God's order of procedure in the working out of His great purpose. Accordingly there is first the *natural humanity* and afterward the *spiritual humanity*; first the *natural birth* and afterward the *spiritual birth*; first the *natural* or earthly *Israel, Zion, temple, priesthood, sacrifices* &c., and afterward their *spiritual* and heavenly counterparts.

If therefore, there were nothing but this passage to guide us, it would be safe to conclude, in the absence of an express statement of Scripture to the contrary, that there is to be no reversal of God's settled order of procedure, no going back from the spiritual to the natural. Hence there can be no return hereafter to the natural Israel, the earthly Jerusalem and the earthly temple, with its smoking altar, its Aaronic priesthood and its animal sacrifices.

It will probably be agreed by all Bible teachers that there is no prediction in the New Testament of a national restoration of the Jewish people; and we believe it has been already shown in these pages that the testimony of the New Testament excludes the possibility of such a thing. Further proof to the same effect will be found below. But it is thought by some that there is a hint of the national restoration of Israel in the following Scriptures:

1. The Lord Jesus Christ, in warning His disciples of the then approaching doom of Jerusalem and the Jewish nation, said:

"And they shall fall by the edge of the sword, and shall be led away captive into all nations; and Jerusalem shall be trodden down of the Gentiles *until the times of the Gentiles be fulfilled*" (Lu. 21:24).

2. The apostle Paul, in dealing with the very question we are now considering, namely, "*Hath God cast away His people?*" (Rom. 11:1), says:

"For I would not, brethren, that ye should be ignorant of this mystery, lest ye should be wise in your own conceits;

that blindness in part is happened to Israel *until the fullness of the Gentiles be come in*" (Rom. 11:25).

The argument of those who cite the above passages in support of the doctrine of a national future for the Jews is, that the word "until" implies a change of some sort at the expiration of the period indicated, and they jump to the conclusion that the implied change is that which their doctrine calls for. But obviously, even if a change of some sort is implied by the word "until," it by no means follows that the change will be in the national status of the scattered people; or that it will take place in a yet future era. Strictly speaking, the word "until" gives not the slightest indication as to *what* will take place when the period which the passage limits shall have run its course. What that word declares, and all it declares, is that throughout "the times of the Gentiles" Jerusalem will be trodden down of the Gentiles, and that spiritual blindness, which has been laid as a punishment upon the greater part of the natural Israel, will persist until the fullness of the Gentiles be come into the fold of Christ.

But before inquiring what room is left by these Scriptures for a possible season of special mercy to those of Jewish descent, let us take note of the purpose for which they are apparently written.

What has chiefly impressed the writer when meditating upon the above Scriptures is that they constitute (and were specially designed to that end) a two-fold testimony to the authenticity of the Scriptures, a testimony which has this remarkable character, namely, *that it was to be before the eyes of every generation of men throughout the entire Christian era.* Here are two distinct predictions, one concerning the City of Jerusalem, the other concerning the Jewish people; predictions of such sort that, had they been the utterances of men, would long since have failed. They are, moreover, predictions that have required for their age-long fulfilment *two continuing miracles*; first, that Jerusalem should be preserved from destruction and yet should be trodden down of the Gentiles throughout the entire era; and second, that the Jewish race should be preserved and be everywhere recognizable – not amalgamated with other races – though scattered throughout the world and commingled with other peoples for centuries of time.

114

To all who reflect upon these truly miraculous facts and are willing to allow them their proper probative value, it will be evident, and apart from all other proofs, that the New Testament is indeed of Divine Authorship. For truly, these are stupendous miracles; and moreover, they are unique among the miracles of the Bible in that they have the character of *continuance*. Every successive generation has witnessed the remarkable fact that Jerusalem, though bereft of its proper inhabitants, has not shared the fate of other cities of antiquity – Babylon, Nineveh, Tyre and Sidon; and has witnessed also the companion fact that the Jewish people, in defiance of all natural law and contrary to all human experience, has not been absorbed into other races or exterminated by the fierce persecutions they have suffered, but have maintained their racial identity and have even thriven and multiplied during the nineteen hundred years of their dispersion throughout the world.

Surely the Book that foretold such unlikely happenings concerning a people and their dearly cherished city, sundered apart the one from the other, must be divinely inspired; and in this may be clearly seen the purpose of the above quoted passages. But regardless of this purpose, it is plain that, in neither passage, is there so much as a hint to the effect that there is to be, at the termination of the times of the Gentiles, a "dispensation" in which the Jewish nation is to be revived and re-established in the land of Canaan; in which Jerusalem is to become the political head and the religious center of a densely populated and completely pacified world; and in which the temple is to be rebuilt, its priesthood and animal sacrifices restored, &c., &c., as currently taught.

It cannot be too strongly insisted or too firmly maintained that the doctrine of a coming millennial age of Jewish supremacy on earth, an age in which nations of men are to be saved with a salvation different in kind from, and distinctly inferior to, gospel salvation, is *a thoroughly unscriptural and anti-scriptural doctrine*. It cannot be too strongly insisted or too firmly maintained that there is *no going backward* in the works of God; that *He* does not build again the things *He* has destroyed; that there is *no* salvation for Jew or Gentile other than *gospel-salvation*; that there is no day of salvation for any part of the human race except *this present day of gospel mercy for all*; that there is no "Israel" in God's purpose but

115

"the Israel *of God*," and no "Zion" but that heavenly mount to which *we* "are come"; and finally, that the temporal shadows of the old covenant – the temple, altar, priesthood, sacrifices and ordinances – have now been abolished completely and forever. The current doctrine as to the conditions of things in the world during the millennium has no biblical foundation. It is a hybrid; the product of a commingling of heathen superstition and corrupted Judaism. To this subject we will come in our last chapter.

From the above it follows, that there is but one form the mercy of God to the Jewish people can possibly assume. It must take the form of *gospel-salvation*; and hence it must come in this present "day of salvation," or not come at all.

All this being understood, it yet remains that the passage in Romans 11:25 leaves room for, even if it does not imply, a time to come during this gospel era when the supernatural blindness, imposed as a punishment upon the Jews as a nation, will be removed, or at least abated, so that the gospel message will have a far greater effect among them than during the time the veil was upon their hearts, and that many of them may be saved. Paul's heart's desire and prayer to God for Israel was "that they might be saved"; and it is reasonable to assume that, in so praying, he was "praying in the Holy Ghost." This lends support to the expectation that there will yet be a mighty working of the Spirit and the word of God amongst the Jewish people, something analogous to "the latter rain" – in which, of course, Gentiles too will participate.

It is apparent upon an attentive perusal of Romans IX-XI that the subject of a national restoration for the Jews is not in contemplation at all. What occupies the apostle's mind is the distressing "mystery" (11:25) of Israel's failure to recognize the promised Messiah when He came to them, and to receive the salvation He offered them. The salvation of God, foretold by the prophets and now proclaimed by the gospel (1 Pet. 1:9-12), is what Israel as a nation had "not obtained," though they had been seeking for it (Rom. 11:7); for truly they had been eagerly looking for what their expected Messiah was to bring them and do for them, though all but a very small remnant were wholly mistaken as to the nature of the salvation foretold by the prophets (See Chapter XVI herein).

Incidentally it may be well to point out that the chief item or feature of God's salvation is *"the righteousness of God,"* "which is, by faith of Jesus Christ, upon all them that believe; for there is no difference" (Rom. 3:22); and this is the chief feature of the Kingdom of God, as defined in Chap. 14:17; for the Kingdom of God is salvation, and that Kingdom is what Israel as a people had ever been seeking for (though they utterly misunderstood the nature of it) and which the elect remnant in Paul's day had already "obtained."

THE FIGURE OF THE OLIVE TREE

At verse 14 of Chapter 11 Paul again refers to those of his own flesh and again gives voice to his intense desire that he "might save some of them." And he goes on to say: "For if the casting away of them be the reconciling of the world, what shall the receiving of them be but life from the dead?" (v. 15). The words "receiving of them," following the words "the casting away of them," indicate that Paul was not without hope that numbers of Jews might yet "be saved"; and then, in the verses that follow (vv. 17-24) he illustrates by the figure of the olive tree what God's salvation does for Jews and Gentiles alike, and how the true Israel is composed.

We do not attempt an exposition of those verses, it being necessary only to point out that the Israel of God's eternal purpose is here represented by an olive tree, whereof the branches are holy because the root is holy (see Psalm 52:8); that the salvation of Gentiles is represented as having the effect of grafting them (who by nature were the branches of a wild olive tree) into that "good olive tree," thereby making them fellow-partakers of *the root* (Christ) and *the fatness* (the Holy Spirit, commonly typified in Scripture by the oil derived from the olive) of that tree; and finally that the unconverted Jews are represented as branches "broken off" from the olive tree, in other words, as dead sticks fit only for the fire.

Verse 20 tells us it was "because of unbelief they were broken off," but evidently Paul did not regard their state as hopeless; for he says that "they also, if *they abide not still in unbelief,* shall be grafted in; for God is able to graft them in again" (v. 23). Paul is here speaking of the salvation – not merely of an occasional individual, but – of the great mass of the people, represented by the branches broken off from the olive tree.

Thus, while the passage intimates, on the one hand, that there may come a time when the Jews as a whole will be much more receptive of the message of the gospel than they have been during the centuries past, it makes plain, on the other hand, that the only salvation for them is the same olive-tree salvation whereof Gentiles (as well as Jews) who believe in Jesus Christ are made partakers, and that the condition of their being saved is that "they continue not in unbelief."

The words "And so all Israel shall be saved" (v. 26) have been strangely misunderstood. They have been taken to mean that all natural Jews are to be saved in a coming dispensation. But they cannot possibly be made to yield that meaning. The adverb "so" declares *how* (not *when*) "all Israel" shall be saved. It refers to the process of grafting into the good olive tree branches from "a wild olive tree" and branches broken off from the good olive tree itself; and it declares that "so," that is to say, *in that manner*, and hence necessarily *in this present dispensation of the Holy Spirit*, "all" the Israel of God shall be saved. Instead therefore, of indicating a special (earthly) salvation for the Jews in a future dispensation, the words, "And so all Israel shall be saved," preclude all possibility of such a thing.

UNTIL THE FULNESS OF THE GENTILES BE COME IN

When will that be? The advocates of modern dispensationalism seem to take for granted that it will be the very end of the gospel era, the very last day of grace. If that be indeed the sense, then either the blindness laid upon the Jewish people will *never* be removed, or else their deliverance from that spiritual blindness will take place in a future era. But I cannot conceive that, if the apostle had intended to express either of those meanings, he would have chosen the words of the text for that purpose. When he wished to indicate (as many times he did) the end of the day of salvation, he always did it by words of clear import; whereas manifestly the words "until the fulness of the Gentiles be come in," are most inappropriate for the purpose.

Rather do they indicate a coming season, of longer or shorter duration, when gospel work among the nations will have been substantially ended and the great mass of those that have been ordained unto eternal life will have been reached and saved; leaving a few here and there to be gathered in, two or three berries in the top of the uppermost bough, four or five in the outmost branches (Isa. 17:6).

It may mean (and I think does mean) that, just as there was at the beginning a short season that was distinctly Jewish (during which, however, some Gentiles were saved), and then a much longer season that has been distinctly Gentilish (although some Jews were saved during its course), so will there be at the end another period distinctly Jewish in character, during which, however, there will be some Gentiles brought into the Kingdom.

In yet another passage, written to Gentile Christians, (2 Cor. 3:12-18) Paul speaks of the spiritual blindness that had fallen upon the great mass of the Jewish people. Referring to the Old Covenant, which was but temporary, and comparing it with the New Covenant, which abides forever, the apostle recalls the occasion when Moses put a veil over his face, thereby foreshowing that the children of Israel would be unable to see "the end of that (covenant) which is abolished." And he adds: "But their minds were blinded; for until this day remaineth the same veil untaken away in the reading in the reading of the Old Covenant; which veil is done away (for them who are) in Christ. But even unto this day, when Moses is read, the veil is upon their heart" – blinding them to the fact that the Mosaic covenant is come to an end (and it is so even to this day, nineteen hundred years later) – "Nevertheless when it (the heart) shall turn to the Lord, the veil shall be taken away."

This passage seems to imply, or at least it leaves room for, a coming time when the heart of natural Israelites will "turn to the Lord" on a scale not hitherto witnessed. And this brings to mind the last words spoken by Moses to that people, in which, after warning them of what would befall them in the latter days because of their manifold sins and persistent disobedience, he said that nevertheless,

119

if they would call to mind his words among all the nations whither the Lord their God should have driven them, and would "return unto the Lord" and "obey His voice," then He would turn their captivity and have compassion on them (Deut. 20:1-3).

To the writer's mind the foregoing is a far more glorious and worthy fulfilment of the promises of blessing to Israel, and a far more satisfactory interpretation of the prophecies, than what are obtained by the imagining of a millennium of earthly bliss with a reconstituted Jewish nation at the head of God-fearing Gentiles, all satiated with material prosperity and going up year by year to keep the feast of tabernacles at Jerusalem.

In concluding our remarks upon this part of our subject, we would point out that, conditions being what they are, the work of converting a multitude of Jews to Christ might be only a matter of days. For the millions of Jews now living, though scattered through all the nations of the world, are nevertheless in touch with one another through various organizations and societies, and are bound together by ties that have marvelously resisted the tooth of time and all the destructive influences of the world. Moreover, they are all located at, or are in easy reach of, one or another of *the centers of Christian civilization*; which means that they all have ready access to the word of the gospel. And finally, the facilities for swift communication by train, airplane, telegraph, wireless and radio, have been wonderfully developed within a few decades past; and it is as least possible that these may be what are represented by the horses and chariots and litters and swift beasts seen in the vision of the prophet who, looking on the days just preceding new heavens and the new earth, speaks first of those saved Israelites whom God would send "unto the nations," and who, says He, "shall declare My glory among the Gentiles" (Isaiah 66:19); and then adds: "And they (the Gentiles) shall bring all your brethren for an offering unto the Lord *out of all nations* upon horses and in litters (*marg.* coaches) and upon mules, and upon swift beasts, to My holy mountain Jerusalem, saith the Lord, as the children of Israel bring an offering in a clean vessel into the house of the Lord" (v. 20).

CHAPTER XIV

"THE HOPE OF THE GOSPEL." CHRIST'S PERSONAL TEACHING

In a previous chapter it was pointed out, from the repeated utterances of the apostle Paul recorded in the last six chapters of Acts, that "the hope of Israel" is identical with "the hope of the gospel," which hope is, of course, the resurrection. We recall that to the Jews at Rome Paul said: "For this cause therefore have I called for you, to see you and to speak with you; because that *for the hope of Israel* I am bound with this chain" (Acts 28:20).

What he had preached as *the hope of Israel* is clearly stated in previous chapters of Acts. Thus, in chapter 23:6 he had said, "Of *the hope and resurrection of the dead* I am called in question" (see also 24:14,15). And in replying to his accusers before Herod Agrippa he said: "And now I stand and am judged for *the hope of the promise made of God unto our father, unto which our twelve tribes* instantly (or intently) serving God day and night *hope* to come. *For which hope's sake*, King Agrippa, I am accused of the Jews. Why should it be though a thing incredible with you *that God should raise the dead?*" (Acts 26:6-8). And in the same address he solemnly affirmed that in all his testimony, both to small and great, he had said "none other things than those which the prophets and Moses did say should come" (v. 22).

Thus the apostle proclaimed everywhere, both by word of mouth and by letter, that there is but *one hope* for all mankind, a hope which indeed had been promised by the O.T. Scriptures *to Israel only*, but which, according to the now revealed "mystery of Christ," is preached to Gentiles equally with Jews. He taught that just as there is but "one faith" for both Jew and Gentile, so likewise there is but "one hope of your calling" (Eph. 4:4), which "calling" (as Chapters I-III were written specially to show) embraces both Jews and Gentiles upon identically the same terms (Eph. 3:6).

This, however, was directly contrary to the doctrine of the scribes and rabbis. According to their carnal interpretation of the Scriptures the promises concerning "Israel," which Paul applied to a *spiritual* people, were to have a *material* fulfilment; and "the hope of Israel," according to them, was the national restoration of the Jewish people. The difference between "the hope of Israel" as held and taught by them, and "the hope of Israel," as preached by Paul, was so radical as to arouse against him their bitterest hatred, insomuch that they denounced him to the civil authorities and plotted to take his life.

ANOTHER HOPE

In view of these facts, so clearly set forth in the Acts and Epistles, it is a matter of deep concern that in our day there has been a revival (and that among evangelical groups of Christians) of the preaching of a distinct and different hope for the natural descendants of Jacob. Thus the preaching of the one and only gospel, with its "one hope" for all mankind, the only gospel and the only hope preached or recognized by the apostles, has been so far set aside in our day as to make room for the very same hope which the Jewish teachers held in Paul's day. And not only so, but our modern teachers support this radically different "hope of Israel" by the very same process of carnalizing the O.T. prophecies and promises which Paul denounced and refuted in his day. It was for this cause that he suffered persecution and imprisonment; for it is certain that, had Paul preached the same "hope of Israel" that is now commonly preached from orthodox periodicals, he would have been honored by his fellow countrymen, rather than persecuted.

NOT IN THE NEW TESTAMENT

It is admitted by those who teach a distinct hope for the Jewish nation apart from the "one hope" of the gospel, that there is nothing in the N.T. to support that doctrine. They admit that the N.T. will be searched in vain for any statement to the effect that, when the day of grace is ended and the Lord Jesus Christ is revealed from heaven in flaming fire, He will convert the whole Jewish nation then on earth, and re-establish them in Palestine.

This admission that the doctrine we are discussing is not found in the N.T. is fatal to it. For the prophecies concerning the second coming of Christ, recorded in the Gospels, Epistles, and Revelation, are so full and detailed that, if the national restoration of the earthly Israel were part of the program of the second advent, it would most certainly have been clearly set forth therein. And beyond all doubt Paul would have mentioned it in the eleventh chapter of Romans, where he speaks distinctly of the future of Israel. Moreover, he would surely have proclaimed it when put on trial as to his teaching *concerning this very matter*, first before the Sanhedrin at Jerusalem, and then successively before Felix, Festus, and Agrippa. We have seen that on all those four occlusions the apostle maintained, and at the peril of his life, that the "hope of Israel" was *a radically different thing* from what the Jewish leaders supposed.

For those who accept the teaching of Paul this should be decisive of the question we are now examining. But we propose to go further than this, and to show that the doctrine of national restoration for the Jewish nation at the beginning of the next dispensation, is *directly contrary* to the plain teaching of the New Testament as a whole. And if we can show this, then it must be contrary to the O.T. also; since there can be no disagreement between the two.

The present writer received the doctrine of the future restoration of "Israel after the flesh" as part of a system of teaching which he accepted *in bulk* because of the soundness and excellence of reputation of those who sponsored it. But, having now learned to his sorrow and mortification that he has held and taught error of a serious kind, it is his duty thus to confess it, and also to do what in him lies to establish the truth of the matter.

NO SECOND CHANCE

In the first place then, we affirm with all possible emphasis that for those who now reject the offer of God's mercy in the gospel of His grace there is *no second chance*. This is the truth of God as revealed in every part of the New Testament. It applies to Jews and Gentiles alike; for there is absolutely "no difference" of any sort, kind, or description. All are in precisely the same condemnation;

and likewise, to each and all, the gospel of Christ offers precisely the same salvation, with *precisely the same eternal consequences for all who refuse it*. "For," says the apostle, "we have before proved *both Jews and Gentiles* that they are *all under sin*" (Rom. 3:9) and from that starting point of perfect equality in guilt ("*all the world* guilty before God") he proceeds to declare the *one ground* of pardon *for all*, "the redemption that is in Christ Jesus," and the *one condition* upon which it is bestowed, "through faith in His blood" (Rom. 3:23-25).

Moreover, the apostle shows in this very passage that the true meaning of God's promise to Abraham was not that his *natural* seed should possess the land of Canaan, but that his *spiritual* seed (believing Jews and believing Gentiles forming one family) should share with him "the promise that he should be the heir of *the world*" (Rom. 4:13-17; and cf. Rom. 8:17). And finally he shows that the promise was to be fulfilled in the resurrection of Jesus Christ from the dead (4:24,25).

According to the modern teaching we are now discussing, those who are saved through the gospel are forthwith incorporated into the church, which is the body of Christ, and these will be in the highest sphere of blessing and glory hereafter; and those who reject Christ now, *if Gentiles*, will be lost finally and forever, but *if Jews*, they will be *converted in a body at some time subsequent to the second coming of Christ*. Now we are quite at a loss to perceive wherein this doctrine differs from that of "Russellism," or "Millennial Dawn," excepting that the second chance which the former limits to the natural descendants of Jacob, is by the latter extended to all mankind. Indeed we think the view of the Russellites would be easier to support from Scriptures than the other; seeing that it is at least consistent with the principle that God is no respecter of persons, and that all natural and national distinctions have been forever abolished by the cross of Christ.

But to the entire doctrine of another chance, whether to all mankind, or to a select portion of the human race only, we oppose the plain and unimpeachable truth of the Scriptures that, in "the day of God, Who will render *to every man* according to his deed" (Rom. 2:5,6) there will be *no salvation or mercy for any who reject God's*

124

offer of pardon and life now. We affirm that, in that day, so far from there being any special salvation for the Jew, God will visit "indignation and wrath, tribulation and anguish, upon *every* soul of man that doeth evil, OF THE JEW FIRST, and also of the Gentile" (id. vv. 8,9). We affirm that "now is the accepted time, and *now* is the day of salvation"; and there is no other day or hour of salvation for any individual, or for any section of the human race. We affirm that, since the sacrifice of Jesus Christ upon the cross, and by reason thereof, God now recognizes no man after the flesh; and particularly that the old covenant and everything connected with it, including the forfeited promise and hope of earthly blessing to Israel after the flesh (which when given was conditioned upon faithfulness and obedience on their part) has been abolished finally and forevermore.

Does the New Testament teach that "Israel after the flesh" will be converted after the second coming of Christ? and will be then reconstituted as an earthly nation, and re-established as such in Palestine? Or does it, on the contrary, teach that Christ's coming the second time will be for the eternal salvation of all those who look for Him (whether by nature they were Jews or Gentiles), and for the eternal condemnation of all, both Jews and Gentiles, who have not believed on His Name? Does it teach that there will be given to the Jews, after the ending of the day of grace, another opportunity to believe on Him and be saved from the wrath to come, and opportunity from which they who are by nature Gentiles will be excluded? Will the coming "day" be one of mingled wrath and mercy? The former for all unbelievers who are Gentiles in the flesh, and the latter for unbelievers who are Jews in the flesh? These questions truly are of great moment; and it must be that clear answers to them can be found in the New Testament Scriptures. We shall seek them first in ...

THE PERSONAL TEACHING OF CHRIST

Matthew 13:24-30; 36-43. This passage contains the parable of the Tares of the Field. Its teaching on the subject of our inquiry is plain; for the meaning of the parable is explained by the Lord Himself. Its emphasis is upon what will happen at the end of the age. Two classes of people are now mingled together in the world, even as wheat and tares are mingled together in the same field. That state of things is to continue "until the harvest," and "the harvest is the end of the age." At that time there will be a complete separation of the tares and the wheat. The tares will be gathered together and bound in bundles to burn them. This will be done "first"; but the wheat will be gathered into the garner (v. 30). The tares include all who are not "the children of the kingdom," that is to say, all who, whether Jews or Gentiles, have not been regenerated by receiving "the good seed" of the gospel.

In thus teaching that the day of judgment will begin by an outpouring of the fiery wrath of God, which will consume all the wicked, this parable is in perfect agreement with the voice of the whole Scripture from beginning to end. What then is the source, and what can be the purpose and effect, of this modern doctrine which makes an exception in favor of an entire race of men, and that upon the ground of natural descent only? The Lord's words are plain. They admit of *no* exception. And moreover, they were spoken directly into *Jewish* ears, and were intended primarily as a warning to a *Jewish* audience. "As therefore the tares are gathered and burned in the fire; so shall it be in the end of this world. The Son of man shall send forth His angels, and they shall gather out of His Kingdom all things that offend, and *them that do iniquity*; and shall cast them into *a furnace of fire*: there shall be weeping and gnashing of teeth. *Then* shall the righteous shine forth in the Kingdom of their Father."

Thus the Lord has made it plain that the judgment of the wicked will be simultaneous with, *if not anterior to*, the manifestation of the children of God in glory. And by the testimony of many Scriptures it is clearly established that the manifestation of the sons of God is at the same moment with the manifestation of the Lord Jesus Christ Himself. Thus it is written that, "When Christ, who is our life shall appear, *then shall ye also appear with Him in glory*" (Col. 3:4). Again it is written: "When He shall appear *we shall be like Him*" (1 John 3:2). See also to the same effect 1 Corinthians 15:51,52; and 1 Thessalonians 4:14.

John the Baptist had already preached the same warning concerning "the wrath to come" to the many Jews who had flocked to his preaching, saying that He who was to come after him would baptize them with the Holy Ghost (at the beginning of the dispensation of grace) and *with fire,* "Whose fan," said he, "is in His hand, and He will thoroughly purge His floor, and gather His wheat into the garner; but He will burn up the chaff with unquenchable fire." (Matt. 3:11,12).

Thus from the very first, and to *exclusively Jewish audiences,* it was proclaimed that there was but one salvation for all; and that when the day of grace was ended, there would be an immediate and final separation of the saved from the lost.

The foregoing Scriptures therefore completely refute the doctrine of a special salvation for the Jewish nation after the manifestation of the Lord Jesus Christ in glory.

Matthew 16:24-28. In this passage the Lord taught His disciples (all Jews) that for a man's salvation it was necessary that he should take up his cross and follow Him *now.* "For," said He, "the Son of man shall come in the glory of His Father, with His angels, and *then* He shall reward *every man according to His works.*" There will be no mercy or grace to any unsaved ones after that. This teaching is amplified by the Lord in Matthew 25:31-46, as will be presently shown.

Luke 17:20-37. The Lord here replies to the question put to Him by the Pharisees, "when the kingdom of God should come." He tells them first that the kingdom was not coming *then* ("*cometh* not") with outward display, but was already in fact in the midst of them (though they knew it not). But He goes on to speak of the coming of that kingdom in power and glory. The coming of His Kingdom in its future aspect will be "as the lightening, that lighteneth out of one part under heaven, and shineth unto the other part under heaven."

And now let us attend carefully to what follows; for here we have teaching of the clearest sort upon the subject of our inquiry. Our Lord's second coming will be in circumstances like unto those in the days of Noah, and those of the days of Lot. And the resemblance lies in this, namely, that like as, in both those epochs of impending judgment, men in general pursued with entire unconcern their ordinary occupations, as if things were to go on in that way forever,

127

even so shall it be "in the day when the Son of man is revealed." And what then? There shall be an *immediate and final separation.* "There shall be two men in one bed; the one shall be taken (to a place of safety, as was Noah and Lot in his) and the other left (for the outpouring of God's wrath). Two women shall be grinding together; the one shall be taken, and the other left. Two men shall be in the field; the one shall be taken, and the other left."

The significance of the words "taken" and "left" appears clearly from the context, which tells that Noah and his family were *taken away* in safety, and all the rest of the world *left* for judgment; and so likewise in the case of Lot and his wife and daughters. And the whole point of the lesson is that the judgment, which destroyed "*all*" that were left, came upon *the very same day* that those who believed God's warnings were saved. For the words are: "until *the day* that Noah entered into the ark, and the flood came, and destroyed them *all*" (v. 27); and again, "But *the same day* that Lot went out of Sodom, it rained fire and brimstone from heaven, and destroyed them *all*" (v. 29). And then, to put the matter beyond all doubt, the Lord adds these words: "Even thus shall it be *in the day when the Son of man is revealed*" (v. 30).

Is not this teaching, which comes to us from our Lord's own lips, as clear as words can make it? How then say some among us that, so far from the coming of sudden and everlasting judgment in that day upon all who are not in the place of safety which God's grace has provided, that is, "the kingdom of His dear Son" (Col. 1:13), the entire Jewish nation will then look upon Him whom they pierced, will be granted repentance unto life, and will be saved from the coming wrath?

As will be pointed out more fully below, the apostle Peter repeats this teaching of Christ in his second Epistle (Chapter III) laying special emphasis upon the *unexpectedness* of Christ's second coming and of the prominence in those last days of a class of leaders who would speak derisively of "the promise of his coming."

Luke 19:11-27. In this parable also our Lord declares what will happen at His second coming. The part which bears upon our present inquiry is what He says as to the way He will at that time deal with His "citizens," who had hated Him and sent after Him a defiant message, saying, "We will not have this Man to reign over us." This passage is specially pertinent because the description of those "citizens" applies specially to the unbelieving Jews (comp. Psa. 2:1-3, and Acts 4:25). Does He say that He will then reveal Himself to them in grace, and convert the nation in a body? On the contrary, His words are: "But those mine enemies, which would not that I should reign over them, bring hither, *and slay them before me.*"

Matthew 22:1-13. This passage contains the parable of the wedding supper, in which our Lord foretells the course of the preaching of the gospel and its results. There is no need to speak of the details of the parable. It suffices for our present purpose that the doom pronounced upon the man who had not on the wedding garment is regarded by commentators of every school as revealing what will be the fate of all, Jews and Gentiles, who refuse the garment of salvation which is now offered in the gospel.

Matthew 24:36-44. In this passage our Lord repeats to His own disciples the teaching He had previously given to the Pharisees (Lu. 17:20-37). The point He emphasizes is that even His own people will not be warned beforehand of the approach "of that day and hour." "For as in the days that were before the flood, they were eating and drinking, marrying and giving in marriage, *until the day* that Noah entered into the ark, and *knew not* until the flood came, *and took them all away; so shall also the coming of the Son of man be...* Watch therefore, for *ye* know not what hour *your Lord* doth come."

Matthew 25:31-46. This passage contains the most complete statement our Lord has given as to what will take place "when the Son of man shall come in His glory, and all the holy angels with Him." As in all His teaching on this subject, the *first thing* is the separation of all human beings into two companies. For "then shall He sit upon the throne of His glory; and before Him shall be gathered *all nations*; and He shall *separate them* one from another, as a shepherd divideth his sheep from the goats." By some expositors it is thought that our Lord is here speaking only of those living on earth at the time of His coming; and we will take it that way, since it is immaterial, for the purpose of the present inquiry, what view of the scene is adopted. Let it be noted, however, that the separation is by individuals, not *by nations*. All the "sheep" are put on one side, and all the "goats" on the other. The two companies are separated, not according to nationality, but according to the nature of the individuals, *as manifested by their conduct*. To those on the right hand the King shall say, "Come, ye blessed of My Father, inherit the Kingdom prepared for you from the foundation of the world." And to those on His left hand He will say, Depart from Me, ye cursed, into *everlasting fire*, prepared for the devil and his angels." Here again we have a clear statement that the judgment then pronounced will be "everlasting."

Those on His right hand, the "sheep," are evidently His own people. "My sheep," He calls them in John 10:27. It is His "one flock" (John 10:16, Gr.); and so here we are given to foresee the fulfilment of His precise promise, "Fear not, *little flock*, for it is your Father's good pleasure *to give unto you the Kingdom*" (Lu. 12:32). His sheep hear His voice; and these who stand on His right hand in that day have manifested that they are His sheep by obeying His law of love.

But those on His left hand have manifested by their conduct that they are not His; for they have repudiated His authority and His law. There is perfect harmony here with the teaching recorded in Luke 19:11-27; for the conduct of those whom He here bids "depart from Me," plainly said "We will not have this Man to reign over us." There is perfect harmony also with the teaching of Paul in 2 Thessalonians 1:5-10 (to which reference will be made more particularly later on) where he tells of the coming of the Lord to *punish* "with *everlasting* destruction *from the presence* of the Lord, and from the glory of His power," those that "Know not God, and that *obey not the gospel* of our Lord Jesus Christ." In both passages the occasion described is the coming of *the kingdom* in *power* and *glory*; and the eternal blessedness or misery of the individual man in that day will depend upon whether or not he has *obeyed the gospel*. The righteous will then receive the long promised Kingdom, "the Kingdom of God for which ye also suffer" (2 Th. 1:5). But for the rejecters of Christ and His gospel, there is "everlasting punishment" (shall be *punished* with *everlasting* destruction"), away "*from* the presence of the Lord" (note His own words, "Depart *from Me*, ye cursed").

Some have gone far astray in regard to the words: "Inasmuch as ye have done it unto one of the least of these, *My Brethren*, ye have done it unto Me." For, in order to make the passage agree with the doctrine of a special judgment-day salvation for the Jewish nation, the idea has been advanced that, by "My brethren," our Lord meant the *Jewish people* (whom he had stigmatized as "children of the devil," and as a "generation of vipers"), and that living nations would be blessed or cursed in that day, according as they had treated the Jews well or ill. But how can there be any uncertainty as to those whom He is not ashamed to call "Brethren" (Heb. 2:11)? For, in this same Gospel is the record of His own answer to the question, "Who is My mother? and who are My brethren?" He Himself asked that question; and thereupon He stretched forth His hand toward His disciples and said, "Behold My mother and My brethren! For whosoever shall *do the will of My Father* which is in heaven, the same is My brother, and sister, and mother" (Matt. 12:46-50). This makes it quite clear; and all Scripture agrees, that those He is not ashamed to call "Brethren," whom He Himself has sanctified and brought to the Father (Heb. 2:10,11) are they who have *received Him by faith*. For "as many as *received Him*, to them gave He power to become the sons of God, even to them that believe on His Name" (John 1:12).

CHAPTER XV
OTHER N.T. PASSAGES ON THE FUTURE OF ISRAEL

We have now shown by the teaching of our Lord Jesus Christ Himself that at His coming again (of which premonitory sign will be given) there will be an immediate separation of those who have obeyed the gospel from those who have refused its proffered mercy; that the former will enter at once into everlasting glory and blessing and the latter into eternal wrath and judgment. We come now to:

THE TEACHING OF PAUL

Reference has already been made to the passage in Romans 2:1-16, which states that they who in this day of salvation despise the riches of God's goodness, refusing to repent, are even now treasuring up from themselves against the day of wrath; and that just as in this era of grace, the gospel is "to the Jew *first*" (1:16), even so in that day of judgment, the tribulation and anguish upon every soul of man that doeth evil will also be to "the Jew *first*." And the reason is given, namely, that "there is *no respect of persons with God*" (2:9-11). This Scripture alone, if there were no other, would suffice to overthrow completely the doctrine of a special salvation for the natural descendants of Jacob after the day of grace shall have ended, and the day of judgment shall have begun.

Romans 11:1-32. We have already given consideration to this chapter of Romans; and we have seen that it is part of a passage (Chaps. ix-xi) in which the apostle expounds the course of God's dealings with the Jews, in whom he had the deepest and most loving interest, seeing that they were his own "Kinsmen according to the flesh" (9:3). It contains a strong intimation that it lay in the purpose of God, at some time in the then future, to extend special mercy to the Jews (11:24,26,31). The time of this promised visitation is indicated in a general way by the words, "That blindness in part is happened to Israel *until the fulness of the Gentiles be come in*" (11:25). But it is plainly declared that the promised mercy will take the form, *not of a special national salvation after this day of grace* *shall have ended*, but of the incorporating of individual Jews ("natural branches") into the very same "olive tree" (*The Israel of God*), whose "root" is Christ and whose "fatness" is the Holy Spirit (cf. Gal. 3:14) into which believing Gentiles are now being incorporated. It follows, therefore, and other Scriptures (such as those heretofore cited) shut us up to the same conclusion, that the promised visitation of the Jews in mercy must take place *ere this present day of grace comes to an end*.

In a word, whatever "mercy" (11:31,32) may be in store for the natural Jews, will come to them in this day of grace, and *as individuals*, not in the day of judgment, and as a nation.

The teaching of the apostle Paul on the subject of our present inquiry is found mainly in his two Epistles to the Thessalonians, to which we shall now refer.

1 Thessalonians 4:13-5:9. The first part of this well known passage speaks of the descending of the Lord from heaven with a shout, with the voice of the arch-angel, and the trump of God, whereupon "the dead *in Christ* shall rise first." "Then we, which are alive and remain, shall be caught up together with them in the clouds, to meet the Lord in the air." This is the only sort of salvation that the apostle here (or elsewhere) describes as taking place at the coming of the Lord; and it is expressly limited to those who are already "in Christ." Moreover, the apostle goes on to speak of "the times and seasons" of these great events saying that "the day of the Lord so cometh as a thief in the night." And how will it then fare with those who are not found "in Christ?" He tells us they will be assuring themselves of good things ahead by saying, "Peace and Safety" (just as were those who lived and despised God's warnings in the days of Noah, and in the days of Lot), but that "sudden destruction" shall fall upon them, "and they shall not escape." Verse 9 declares that the alternatives presented to all men are "salvation" and "wrath." And so say all the Scriptures.

2 Thessalonians 1:5-10. We have already pointed out the close argument (extending even to similarity of words) between this passage and that in Matthew XXV, in which our Lord Himself declares what will happen at His coming again. It describes the day that was forseen by Daniel when "the kingdom and dominion, and the greatness of the kingdom under the whole heaven, shall be given to the people of the saints of the Most High" (Dan. 7:27); the day "when the Lord Jesus shall be revealed from heaven with His mighty angels"; and the plain declaration is that He will come "in flaming fire, taking vengeance on them that know not God, and that obey not the gospel of our Lord Jesus Christ; who shall be punished with everlasting destruction from the presence of the Lord, and from the glory of His power." Moreover, it is here declared that this sweeping judgment, embracing all who know not God and obey not the Gospel, will be at the very time "He shall come to be glorified in His saints, and to be admired in all them that believe" (2 Th. 1:7-10). By this passage again we are assured that at our Lord's second coming "all them that believe" will be made sharers of His own glory, and all others will "be punished," by banishment away from His presence, to a place of "destruction" that shall be "everlasting."

It has been already noted, and should be kept in mind, that the unconverted Jews have ever been foremost among the despisers of God's mercy, even in the preceding dispensation, and that they have been most conspicuously the rejecters of Jesus Christ and His gospel. For, by trampling upon the law of God, they brought upon themselves and their children all its curses and judgments. Moreover, from the very beginning they have had the Holy Scriptures which testify of Christ; they have heard every Sabbath day the voices of the prophets, which spake beforehand of His coming, and of all He was to do and suffer; they were the first to whom the risen Christ sent the glad tidings of free salvation through His chosen witnesses, who preached the gospel unto them with the Holy Ghost sent down from heaven; and even in these last days special efforts for their salvation have been made through societies organized and maintained for that sole purpose. How can it be supposed then that this passage, and other Scriptures which speak plainly to the same effect, have no application to those who are of "Israel after the flesh?" And what responsibility do we incur, if we preach a doctrine so contrary to that of Christ and His apostles, especially if thereby any should be encouraged to continue in unbelief, trusting the delusive hope of national salvation in the approaching day of wrath? This passage is most assuredly decisive of the question we are considering; for it declares, in language that is unmistakably plain, what will happen at the end of this gospel era to them that have not obeyed the gospel; and certainly, of all the people of the world, the Jews are most conspicuously those who have not obeyed the gospel.

2 Thessalonians 2:2-12. There are difficulties of a minor character in regard to certain details of this passage; but with respect to the subject of our present inquiry it speaks with a certainty and clearness that leaves nothing to be desired. For it plainly declares that, at the Lord's appearing in glory, "that man of sin, the son of perdition," "that Wicked one" (the antichrist) shall be consumed by the spirit (or breath) of His mouth, and destroyed by the effulgence of His presence (*lit. the epiphany of His parousia*); and further that they who would not receive the love of the truth, whereby they might have been "saved," will have been given over by God Himself to "strong delusion, that they should believe *the* lie" (the original has the definite article); to this end, namely (let the words be carefully observed): "That they all might be damned, who believed not *the truth* (the gospel), but had pleasure in unrighteousness."

This agrees perfectly with Christ's own words concerning the flood, "and took them *all* away." It absolutely excludes the possibility of the salvation after His coming of any who have rejected the gospel previously.

2 Peter 3:1-10. The apostle Peter speaks plainly in this passage concerning the scoffers of the last days who deride the warnings of judgment to come; and he declares that the day of wrath will come suddenly, when the earth, and the works therein shall be burned up. Moreover, what he says about the reason for God's long delay (v. 9) precludes the idea of there being any opportunity for repentance after that day begins. This important passage will be considered more in detail in a subsequent chapter.

Revelation 6:12-17. This vision clearly depicts the great day of the wrath of the Lamb. It has no place in it for the salvation of any racial or other group. Moreover, the captains of industry, the magnates and other great ones of the earth are under no illusions whatever as to the doom that is about to overwhelm them.

Revelation 19:11-21. This passage describes a vision of the things that are about to happen at the second coming of Christ. John says: "And I saw heaven opened, and behold, a white horse; and He that sat upon him was called Faithful and True, and in righteousness He doth judge and make war." The vision shows what Christ will do from the moment He issues forth from the opened heaven down to the complete overthrow of all His enemies, the casting of the beast and the false prophet into the lake of fire, the binding of Satan in the bottomless pit, and the setting up of the thrones of His everlasting Kingdom. He comes to "judge and make war." And in keeping with this purpose, His eyes are as a flame of fire, and out of His mouth goeth a sharp two-edged sword, that with it He should smite the nations. John sees also an angel standing in the sun, who cries with a loud voice to all the fowls of the air, saying, "Come and gather yourselves to the great supper of God, that ye mat eat the flesh of kings, and the flesh of captains, and the flesh of mighty men." There is nothing here (and it would be here if anywhere) concerning any group of people whom Christ converts and saves after His coming. The separation is complete from the moment of His appearing; and the children of men are either in the armies of heaven which "followed Him upon white horses clothed in fine linen white and clean," or they are in that other company which includes "the beast and the kings of the earth, and their armies, gathered together to make against Him that sat on the horse, and against His army." For there are no neutrals in that war. Those that are not for Him are against Him. And the end of those who are not with Him is described in these words: "And the remnant were slain with the sword of Him that sat upon the horse, which sword proceeded out of His mouth; and all the fowls were filled with their flesh" (v. 21).

The two edged sword is the symbol of the Word of God (Heb. 4:12). So we have here a description in symbolic language of the fulfilment of Christ's own prophecy: "And if any man hear My words, and believe not, I judge him not; for I came not to judge the world, but to save the world. He that rejecteth Me, and receiveth not My words, hath one that judgeth him; *the word that I have spoken* (the sword of His mouth) the same shall judge him in the last day" (John 12:47,48). For His word is to them that hear it either a word of eternal life, or a word of eternal judgment. It either saves or damns.

The fowls of the air represent, according to the Lord's explanation of the parable of the sower, the wicked spirits, the agents of the evil one.

This vision, and others described in Revelation, absolutely exclude the possibility of salvation after the beginning of the day of wrath for any who have previously rejected the gospel.

It is appropriate also to remark that there is a noticeable and significant absence, throughout the entire Apocalypse, of all reference to the earthly Zion and earthly Jerusalem. The only holy mountain and city that have part and place in those future scenes of blessedness are that "Mount Sion" to which we have been brought, and "the City of the living God, the heavenly Jerusalem," the "City which hath foundations, whose builder and maker is God," and which is attended by "an innumerable company of angels" (Heb. 11:10; 12:22,23).

THE DISCIPLES' QUESTION IN ACTS I

Acts 1:6-8. Here we have the record of our Lord's last words to His disciples before His ascension. The disciples had at last nerved themselves to ask plainly and directly concerning that which was ever uppermost in their Jewish minds; saying, "Lord, wilt Thou at this time restore again the Kingdom to Israel?" His reply (I quote from Bagster's Interlinear) was:

> "It is not yours to know times or seasons which the Father placed in His own authority; but ye will receive power, the Holy Ghost having come upon you, and ye shall be witnesses to Me both in Jerusalem, and in all Judea and Samaria, and to the uttermost part of the earth."

It is quite possible to read into these words the idea that there was to be, in some future "times or seasons," a restoration of earthly dominion to Israel. In fact the writer himself having accepted these modern "Jewish fables" (Which have become so astonishingly popular of late) held to that idea until he could no longer close his eyes to the fact that, by placing that interpretation upon the passage,

137

he was making it contradict the plain teaching of the entire New Testament.

On the other hand it is not difficult to assign to the words of our Lord, quoted above, a meaning that accords perfectly with the Scriptures we have been examining; and this, of course, is what we are bound to do. A careful consideration and quiet pondering of those words lead to the conclusion that here, as on many other occasions, our Lord simply ignored what was in the minds of His disciples (for His thoughts were not their thoughts, neither were their ways His ways). He might well have administered to them on this occasion the same rebuke He had administered to Peter, when that disciple spoke to Him under the influence of the same Jewish expectation; to whom He said, "Thou art an offence to Me; for thou savourest not the things that be of God, but those that be *of men* (Matt. 16:23). But the course He now took was *to disregard entirely the thought of their hearts*, and simply to impress upon them the fact that their all-engrossing occupation was to be that of bearing testimony to His resurrection from the dead. It was to be their supreme business to proclaim that mighty truth of the gospel to the whole world; and for the accomplishment of that great mission, power would be given them through the coming upon them, in a few days, of the Holy Spirit from heaven.

Moreover, a new order of things was then at hand; for Christ was not henceforth to teach them in person and directly, but indirectly, through the Holy Spirit, Who, as He had already told them, should guide them into all truth (John 16:13). And it is a striking fact that after they had received the baptism of the Holy Spirit *they never again spoke of that sort of a kingdom* (Acts 8:12, 19:8, 20:25; 28:31; Rom. 14:17; 1 Cor. 4:20; 15:50; Col. 1:13; 2 Thess. 1:5; Rev. 1:19; &c.).

It is clear from the wording of the disciples' question that they had no doubt in their minds that the kingdom was to be restored to Israel, the only thing to be settled with them being whether the time of its restoration was then at hand; also there is good reason to believe that their conception of the nature of the expected kingdom did not differ materially from that of their fellow Israelites.

There has been discussion in print recently as to whether the question the disciples put to their risen Lord was "an intelligent question"; and it has been argued in behalf of modern Dispensationalism that the question *was* an "intelligent" one, and that it would follow from the Lord's reply that the kingdom was to be restored to Israel at some time then future.

I agree that the question was intelligent; and indeed deem it a most natural and almost inevitable, question for them to ask; for they, in common with all their compatriots, groaning under the tyranny of Rome's iron yoke, were eagerly awaiting the emancipation of the Jewish people and the re-establishment of the earthly kingdom of Israel. Moreover, they had heard their Master say, "Fear not, little flock, for it is your Father's good pleasure *to give you the kingdom*" (Luke 12:32); and at a later time they heard Him say to the chief priests and elders at Jerusalem, "Therefore I say unto you, The Kingdom of God shall be taken from you and *given to a nation* bringing forth the fruits thereof" (Matt. 21:43). And finally, during those forty days when He had appeared to them from time to time, He had been "speaking of the things pertaining to the Kingdom of God." Hence the question was "intelligent" enough.

But it is needful to remember that there were certain things concerning the Kingdom which He was not ready to make known to them, because they were not as yet ready to receive them; things they were to learn later on through the teaching of the Holy Spirit. The Lord had said to them on the night of His betrayal, "I have yet many things to say unto you, *but ye cannot bear them now*. Howbeit, when He, the Spirit of Truth is come, He will guide you into all truth" (John 16:12-13). Especially the truth as to Israel's relationship to the kingdom was a thing they could not "bear" until baptized by the Spirit; for to natural Jews that truth is unbearable. Also they had yet to learn that "the Kingdom of God is not meat and drink, but righteousness, and peace and joy in the Holy Ghost" (Rom. 14:17).

Accordingly they were given to know, through subsequent revelations of the Holy Spirit, that the promised kingdom was of spiritual character, and that the nation to which it was to be given was – not "Israel after the flesh," but – the true "Israel of God."

Furthermore, the question involved "times and seasons" which *the Father* had put in *His own* power. It is the Father who bestows the kingdom (Lu. 12:12); and it is the Father who determines the times and seasons, as it is written, "When the fulness of the time was come, God sent forth His Son" (Gal. 4:4). Now that "little flock," to which the Father was pleased to give the kingdom, was indeed "Israel"; but the mystery concerning the true "Israel," the flock for which the good Shepherd gave His life, had not as yet been made known to them, "as it is *now* revealed to His holy apostles and prophets by the Spirit" (Eph. 3:1-6).

Also it is to be noted that the "times" of the Gentiles, which had a long course to run, had not yet begun; which is an additional reason why the Lord answered them as He did, thereby putting aside the subject of the bestowal of the kingdom, and fixing their minds upon the coming of the Holy Spirit, who would make the whole matter clear.

Finally, seeing there is but one kingdom in God's purpose, and but one Israel, the passage we are considering (Acts 1:1-6) cannot be interpreted in such manner as lends support to the nationalistic dreams of "Israel after the flesh."

AS TO THE "TRIBULATION SAINTS"

Another feature of the modern doctrine of Judaistic nationalism should receive brief attention. I refer to the idea of many modern dispensationalists that the supposed national conversion of the Jews is to take place not actually in the millennium itself, but at the interval between the coming of Christ *for* His saved people and His coming to the earth *with* them. Those who make the "great tribulation" (Matt. 24:21) a yet future event locate it in this interval, which they commonly refer to as "the tribulation period," and they who are saved in that period (with a salvation much inferior to that now offered through the gospel) are termed "tribulation saints." Hence, according to this view, the supposed conversion and restoration of the Jewish nation is to take place not in the millennium but, in a special "tribulation period," which is to intervene between this present day of grace and the millennial day.

140

But all the above, and the many specific features that go with it, are purely the products of the human imagination. The length of the interval between the catching up of the saints to meet the Lord in the air (I Thess. 4:17) and His appearing with them in glory (Col. 3:4; I Jn. 3:2; Rev. 19:11-14 &c.) is not indicated. There is nothing to show that it will be longer than a day, or part of a day. Indeed the interval itself is not referred to anywhere in the Scriptures. Its existence is entirely a matter of inference from I Thessalonians 4:14-17; it being obvious that there must needs be an interim of *some* length between the taking of the saved (living and raised) away from the earth, and their manifestation with Christ in His "glorious appearing" (Tit. 2:12). But it is taking an unwarranted liberty with the word of prophecy to make that interval a period of many years, and to crowd it with events of transcendent importance; and specially so when it is expressly stated that the change of condition of the Lord's people at that time will be effected "in a moment, in the twinkling of an eye" (I Cor. 15:52).

That there will be any gospel-effort during that interval, or any salvation either of nations or of individuals, is purely a dream. And not only so, but the idea is negated, *first*, by the silence of Scripture in regard thereto; *second*, by the testimony of the very passage from which the interval is inferred, I Thessalonians 4:16-5:9. For it is plainly declared in that Scripture that what "cometh upon" those who are not caught away to meet the Lord is – not salvation, or another opportunity to be saved, but – "*sudden* destruction"; which, according to II Thessalonians 1:8,9, is "*everlasting* destruction from the presence of the Lord." The alternative which the passage presents is "salvation" or "wrath" (I Th. 5:9); and concerning those who have not obeyed the gospel it is plainly declared that "they shall not escape."

The doctrine of another chance for any members of Adam's race, and of a period, long or short, in which there will be preached "another gospel," different from that preached by Paul and all the apostles (I Cor. 15:3,4,11), and particularly that of the conversion and restoration of the Jewish nation, cannot be maintained without setting aside the very passage upon which it is supposedly founded, and all other pertinent Scriptures besides.

Other Scriptures testify quite plainly against the idea of a special salvation for Jews after Christ shall have removed His people from the world. Thus Peter, speaking to a concourse of Jews at Jerusalem, whom he addressed as *"Ye men of Israel,"* recalled to their minds the prophecy of Moses of the coming of Christ as a Prophet like unto himself: concerning Whom Moses said: "And it shall come to pass that every soul, which will not hear that Prophet, *shall be destroyed from among the people."* This tells us – not that after Christ comes for His believing people the Jews will be saved in a body, but – that the first thing on the program of the second advent will be that all Jews who have not believed the gospel will be "destroyed from among the people."

This is in exact agreement with what Christ had taught His Jewish auditors, namely, that at the end of the age the reapers should "gather first the tares and bind them in bundles to burn them" (Matt. 13:30).

This earliest of the utterances of Christ's apostles concerning God's future dealings with the Jews is in striking agreement with what Paul subsequently stated at greater length in Romans XI. Peter declares not that God would utterly destroy or cast off that people, but that those of them who would not believe in Jesus Christ were to be "destroyed *from among* the people"; which would leave only the believing Jews, corresponding to the few "natural branches" of Paul's olive tree, that were not broken off. This word of Peter plainly forbids the expectation of any salvation for Jews after the second coming of Christ.

This proclamation by Peter is in striking agreement with the Lord's answer to the prayer of King Solomon, to whom He said (after promising a reward for fidelity):

"But if ye shall at all turn from following Me, ye, or your children, and will not keep My commandments and My statutes which I have set before you, but go and serve other gods and worship; *then will I cut off Israel out of the land which I have given them*; and this house, which I have hallowed for My Name, will I cast out of My sight; and *Israel shall be a proverb and a byword among all people."*

No recovery is hinted at; and so it is with them to the present day.

CHAPTER XVI
WHERE IS THE PROMISE OF HIS COMING?

The testimony of the apostle Peter has a decisive bearing upon the question under consideration; and his testimony is the more weighty because he was in a special sense the apostle to the Jews (Gal. 2:7,8). Most assuredly therefore, if there were to be hereafter an era of earthly greatness and world-supremacy for a revived and re-constituted nation of Israel, and if that were the hope of Israel, the revelation thereof would be found in the writings of Peter. But the writings of that servant of Christ show conclusively that, not only had he no knowledge of such a future for the Jewish nation, but there is nothing of that sort in the purposes of God.

The testimony we wish particularly to bring to the reader's attention is found in Peter's second Epistle, Chapter III; but before presenting it, we will briefly notice several pertinent matters in his first Epistle.

In 1 Peter 1:7 is a reference to "the appearing of Jesus Christ" and the "praise and honor and glory" that will then be the portion of those who endure successfully the trial of their faith. The apostle had previously referred to the *living hope* of those "strangers... elect according to the foreknowledge of God"; which hope he describes as – *not a place in the millennial earth*, but – "an inheritance incorruptible, and undefiled, and that fadeth not away, reserved *in heaven*" (v. 4). This is the "salvation (that is) ready to be revealed in the last time" (v. 5), and this, he says is "the grace that is to be brought unto you at the revelation of Jesus Christ" (v. 13). Can we think the Holy Spirit would have written thus if the appearing of Jesus Christ were to be followed by a thousand years (or period) of earthly bliss for Jews and Gentiles?

Furthermore, the apostle makes at this point an illuminating statement concerning the general subject of O.T. prophecy, showing that it is not at all what the Jewish rabbis of that time were teaching (and what is taught among Christians today) namely, that it had to do with a future state of earthly glory and dominion for the Jewish nation; but that what was revealed to the prophets of Israel concerning "the sufferings of Christ *and the glory that should follow," were the very same things "which are now reported unto you by them that have preached the gospel unto you with the Holy Ghost sent down from heaven"* (vv. 11,12). And we have seen by the above quotations that those things ("which things the angels desire to look into") are such as leave no room for a millennium of earthly delights. Moreover, were it otherwise, and were such a millennium a part of "the glory that should follow," it certainly would have been mentioned here and in other like passages in the N.T.

Chapter II of this first Epistle brings into view two great results of the sufferings of Christ, namely, *first*, the "spiritual house" that is now being built upon Christ, the "chief Corner Stone, elect precious," laid *in Zion*; and *second*, the "holy nation," which is "a royal priesthood" and "a peculiar people" to God. As has been already pointed out, this passage (I Peter 2:1-9) shows that the "Zion" of unfulfilled prophecy is a *spiritual* locality; that the "temple" of unfulfilled prophecy is a *"spiritual* house," and that the "Israel" that was to inherit the promise of future glory, is that "holy nation," which includes all who have been begotten again unto a living hope by the resurrection of Jesus Christ and have been redeemed by His precious blood.

THE PROMISE OF HIS COMING

Turning now to Peter's second Epistle, we find in Chapter III a prophecy concerning a class of persons, designated "scoffers," who should come upon the scene "in the last days." It is evident, from the attention paid to them in this Epistle, that those "scoffers" would constitute a prominent and highly influential class of persons in the end-times of the gospel era. What would specially distinguish them is the doctrine they would hold, the substance of which is the *gradual and uninterrupted progress of human civilization* (which is the essence of the modern theory of evolution); and on the basis of which doctrine they would deride those Bible prophecies that foretell the sudden and complete destruction of the world, including all the great works whereof men make their boast, at the second coming of Christ. The characteristic attitude of those scoffers of the last days is very plainly revealed by their derisive question: "*Where is the promise of His coming? for since the fathers fell asleep all things continue as they were from the beginning of the creation*" (v. 4).

It is specially to be noted, for the purpose of the present inquiry, that the apostle here contemplates the coming of Christ – not as the beginning of an era of tranquility and prosperity for the earth, but – as the signal for its utter destruction.

Those "scoffers," whose doctrine so strikingly resembles that of present-day evolutionists and modernists, are charged with being "willingly ignorant" of historical facts recorded in the Bible, which show that all things have *not* continued without interruption at the hand of God, and also of Bible prophecies, to the effect that mundane affairs *will not* continue without interruption on His part in the future. Specifically the apostle charges them with being willfully (or willingly) ignorant that the world, which existed in the days of Noah, having been, by the word of God, "overflowed with water, perished"; and that, correspondingly, "the heavens and earth which now are, by the same word are kept in store, reserved *unto fire* against the day of judgment and perdition of ungodly men" (vv. 5-7).

This gives us Peter's outlook for the world that now is, and tells what is to happen to it at the coming again of Jesus Christ – not a millennium of peace and plenty, but total destruction by fire, a destruction comparable to what was accomplished in the days of Noah by the agency of water.

The passage gives us also the Holy Spirit's answer to those who scoff at the promise of the coming again of the Lord Jesus Christ; an answer which manifestly cold not have been given if His coming were to have the effect of changing the present conditions on earth into a millennium of unmixed blessedness.

Then follows (vv. 8,9) the Divine explanation of what appears, from the human standpoint, to be *a long delay on God's part*, evincing the slackness in the fulfilment of His promise. First, the apostle reminds his readers that God, who inhabiteth eternity, does not measure time as man does; for that with Him one day is as a

146

thousand years and a thousand years as one day. And he adds (this being a statement to which special heed should be given) *"The Lord is not slack concerning His promise, as some men count slackness; but is long suffering to us-ward, not willing that any should perish, but that all should come to repentance."*

This verse needs no explanation; for it plainly declares what the preceding verses had distinctly intimated, that at the coming again of Jesus Christ the opportunity for repentance *will end,* and all who have not previously repented will "perish"; just as in the days of Noah all who were not in the ark "perished" (v. 6). It is absolutely impossible, in the light of this verse, to maintain that the entire Jewish nation is to be saved (and many Gentiles also) at the Lord's second coming.

Manifestly, if there were to be, as now is commonly taught, salvation for every Jew in the world, and for Gentiles too, at the second coming of Christ, it could not be said that the delay in His coming is due to the long suffering of God and to His desire that not any should perish.

The apostle then proceeds to declare that, notwithstanding the seeming delay, and notwithstanding the confident assertions to the contrary of the scoffers of the last days, *"the day of the Lord will come"* (v. 10); and moreover he proceeds to tell *how* it will come, and also *what will happen* when it does come.

First be it observed that the apostle speaks of the coming of *Christ* and the coming of *the day of the Lord as one and the same thing.* It is utterly impossible therefore, that a period of a thousand years should intervene between the coming of the Lord Jesus Christ and "the day of the Lord." This makes pre-millennialism of the current type (which is practically the same as that held by the Jew of Christ's day) an impossibility.

Then the apostle declares that the day of the Lord will come as a complete surprise, even "as a thief in the night"; and in so saying, Peter is merely repeating what Christ Himself had declared with great emphasis and particularity. Paul also says the same (I Thess. 2:5) and John likewise (Rev. 3:3). The testimony of Scripture to the effect that the second coming of Christ will be at such a time as will take all men, *His own followers included,* by surprise, is copious and very impressive. And this makes it still further impossible that His coming should be at the end of a millennium of earthly tranquility, peace and prosperity; so that the Scripture we are considering is as fatal to *post*-millennialism, of the type currently held by some, as it is to *pre*-millennialism.

Let us recall some of the plain statements of Scripture touching this transcendently important matter:

> *Matthew 24:47.* "*As the lightning* cometh out of the east and shineth unto the west; so also shall the coming of the Son of man be." (See Luke 17:24).

> *Matthew 24:30,31.* "*They shall see* the Son of man coming in the clouds with power and great glory. And He shall send His angels with *a great sound of a trumpet.*"

> *I Thess. 4:16.* It will be "with *a shout, the voice of the archangel and the trump of God.*"

> *Matt. 24:36-42.* It will be unexpectedly; at a time known only to the Father.

> *I Thess. 5:2,3.* "The day of the Lord so cometh as a thief in the night. For when they shall say, Peace and safety, then sudden destruction cometh upon them."

> *II Thess. 1:7-9.* "The Lord Jesus shall be revealed from heaven with His mighty angels, in flaming fire taking vengeance on them that know not God, and that obey not the gospel – who shall be punished with everlasting *destruction* from the presence of the Lord."

In order to uphold the doctrine of a millennium under Jewish auspices to follow the coming of the Lord, it is necessary to assume that Peter, in writing the above prophecy, purposely overlooked the millennium, passing it over in silence and writing *as if* the next thing following this present age was to be the day of judgment. But what calls for explanation, in order to give plausibility to the above supposition, and what has never been explained to the writer's satisfaction, is how – upon the assumption that this age is to be followed by a millennium of earthly bliss – the apostle Peter, and every other New Testament writer who deals with the subject of Christ's second coming, could write *as if* the day of judgment were to follow immediately hereafter.

That Peter does indeed write as if the next thing after this day of salvation is the day of the Lord, and that every other N.T. writer does the same, is indisputable; and the only reasonable explanation thereof is that they have so written because so it is to be.

Then the apostle delivers an admonition based upon his prediction of what is to happen when Christ comes again, saying: "Seeing then that all these things shall be dissolved, what manner of persons ought ye to be in all holy conversation and godliness, *looking for and hasting unto the coming of the day of God, wherein the heavens being on fire shall be dissolved, and the elements shall melt with fervent heat*" (v. 11,12).

Manifestly, Peter could not have written this admonition if, instead of predicting the day of judgment at the second coming of Christ, he had foretold a millennium of earthly delights; for clearly it is not possible for God's people of this present era to be impressed by the approaching dissolution of the existing heavens and earth and to be "looking for," much less "hasting unto," the day of God, if in fact, and if the word of God elsewhere makes known, that a thousand years are to intervene, during which the earth that now is will exist in a glorified state.

Then Peter says: "Nevertheless we, according to His promise, look for new heavens and a new earth wherein dwelleth righteousness." But manifestly, the new heavens and new earth could not be in the foreground of his expectation, or of ours, if there were to come first a millennium of the Lord's own presence, during which we are to share the glory of His throne. In that case "the coming of the day of God" would be but faintly in view, if at all.

In this connection we should recall the Lord's promise to His disciples that in the regeneration, they should sit on twelve thrones, judging the twelve tribes of Israel. That prospect must have been always before Peter's eyes; and since he here tells us that he according to the Lord's promise, was looking for new heavens and a new earth, it is certain that Christ's promise to his disciples will be fulfilled – not in an earthly millennium, but – in the new creation.

No one, we are sure, could read this passage in 2 Peter with an open mind, and in simple confidence that the word of God is written to enlighten and not to mislead, without being convinced that, at the end of this present day of salvation, *Christ will come again*; and that His coming will be followed immediately *by the day of judgment*, the destruction of the present creation by fire, and the ushering in of the new heavens and new earth. And we say, moreover, that there is not a passage anywhere in the Bible that teaches, or that fairly implies, anything to the contrary; while there are not a few that confirm it.

It is appropriate at this point to turn back a few pages to the Book of Hebrews, and to recall once more that the fathers of Israel were taught, even as the saints of the present era are taught, to look – not for a glorified earth, whereof the earthly Jerusalem is to be the metropolitan city and the religious center, but – "for a city which hath foundations, whose builder and maker is God," and for "a better country, that is an heavenly" (Heb. 11:10 and 16).

Peter's concluding exhortation reiterates the main doctrine of the passage, namely, that "the *longsuffering of our Lord is salvation*"; thus evincing a desire to impress upon the reader's mind that the lapse of time before the fulfilment of the promise of His coming is due to the solemn fact that His coming marks *the very end of the day of salvation*. And Peter continues without a break or new sentence, saying, "*even as our beloved brother Paul also according to the wisdom given unto him hath written unto you; as also in all his epistles, speaking of these things.*"

Let us beware, therefore, of those who would make it appear that Paul, in his Epistles, teaches anything not in perfect harmony with what Peter declares in the passage we have been considering. And let it be recalled at this point that, as has already been shown, Paul also, in his foretelling of the second coming of Christ, gives prominence to the fact that it will be attended by the destruction of the world by fire, and the judgment and perdition of ungodly men. For Paul too looks on to the end of the present order of things; to the time when God will recompense *tribulation* to them who now trouble His people, and to those who now are troubled rest with his apostles; and according to Paul, that will be "*when the Lord Jesus shall be revealed from heaven with His mighty angels, in flaming fire*, taking vengeance on them that know not God and that obey not the gospel of our Lord Jesus Christ, who shall be *punished with everlasting destruction* from the presence of the Lord, and from the glory of His power." And once more we are told that this will be "*When He shall come to be glorified in His saints and to be admired in all them that believe* (because our testimony among you was believed) *in that day* (2 Thess. 1:6-10). Thus we see that, as in Peter's account, so likewise in Paul's the conspicuous features of the events that will attend the coming again of the Lord Jesus Christ from heaven, and the *flaming fire*, and the *everlasting punishment* of the ungodly. Paul identifies these as they "that know not God, and that *obey not the gospel* of our Lord Jesus Christ"; which words make it evident that the events he describes – that is, the awarding of "rest" to God's people and "tribulation" to their enemies – will take place at the end of this day of gospel salvation. "That day" of vengeance will follow next after *this* day of the gospel.

Again we see, as from Peter's description of that coming "day of the Lord's vengeance" (Isa. 34:8), that it is impossible that those events could be preceded by a millennium during which the earth was populated by none but worshippers of God. So this passage in 2 Thessalonians also makes *post*-millennialism (of the commonly held sort) an utter impossibility.

Between the teaching of Paul and that of modern pre-millennialists there is this immense difference: According to the former, all who obey not the gospel of Christ are to be punished, when He comes again, with everlasting destruction *from* His presence; but according to the latter, the Jewish rejecters of the gospel (and others a little later) are to be blessed with a thousand years of undiluted happiness and prosperity *in* His presence. Is it possible to imagine a greater difference than that?

In the endeavor to harmonize this passage (2 Thess. 1:7-10) with the usual pre-millennial teaching, it is sometimes said that the passage refers to a "second stage" of Christ's coming. For according to one of the recent refinements of the doctrine, the one "coming' of our Lord is divided into several "stages," and certain passages are assigned to the first stage, and others, that cannot be made to agree with the interpretation placed upon the first group of Scriptures, to the second stage; it being usual to place the "great tribulation" – which we are told is to last three-and-a-half years – between the two "stages." But, apart from the fact that there is not the slightest warrant for this arbitrary arrangement of passages, which all refer to one and the same coming of the Lord from heaven, the difficulty referred to above is not in the least lessened thereby. For it is impossible to see, in the light of this passage, how any segment of humanity, Jew or Gentile, can be converted and blessed after a first (or any other) stage of the Lord's coming.

Furthermore, to those who give attention to the wording of the passage it will be evident that it relates – not to a later stage, but – to the *very earliest* period of the Lord's second coming. For all are agreed that the first thing on the program of the events of "that day," is the resurrection of "the dead in Christ" and the catching away of all who are His (the living being changed in a moment, in the twinkling of an eye) to meet the Lord in the air. Such is the clear teaching of I Corinthians 15:51,52 and I Thessalonians 4:13017. And it is important (in view of the modern teaching of a "secret rapture") to notice that both the above cited passages make this to be *a world-shaking event*. The first (I Cor. 15:51,52) states that the instantaneous change of all the people of God in the world to the state of immortality, and the simultaneous raising of the dead incorruptible, will be "*at the last trump; for the trumpet shall sound, and the dead shall be raised incorruptible, and we shall be changed.*" And the second passage puts it thus: "For the Lord Himself shall descend from heaven *with a shout, with the voice of the archangel and with the trump of God; and the dead in Christ shall rise first; then we which are alive and remain shall be caught up together with them in the clouds to meet the Lord in the air; and so shall we ever be with the Lord*" (I Thess. 4:13-17).

All are agreed, we believe (and certainly it should be evident to all who give consideration thereto) that these two passages refer to the same coming events. And it seems quite clear also that the passage we have quoted from 2 Thessalonians 1:6-10 refers to the very same events; for the apostle is there speaking of the time when

God will award "rest" to His people, the time of the union of Christ with His saints, when He shall come to be glorified and admired in them. All the passages we have examined, and all others that relate to the subject in hand, agree in testifying that, at the coming again of our Lord from heaven, the day of salvation will end, and the day of eternal "rest" for His people, and of eternal "destruction" for His enemies, will begin.

CHAPTER XVII

"THE ELECTION HATH OBTAINED IT" – HATH GOD CAST AWAY HIS PEOPLE?

The Spirit of God has caused it to be placed on record that –

"Israel hath not obtained that which he seeketh for; but the election hath obtained it" (Rom. 11:7).

Of what is the apostle speaking? What is it Israel was seeking for and had not obtained, but which the election *had obtained and was in possession of*, at the time the Epistle to the Romans was written?

The apostle deemed it not necessary to specify what he had in mind. We may infer it was something so well known that they to whom the Epistle was addressed would understand his meaning without a more explicit statement. And surely, what Israel was expecting was, and is, so well known by all who have any acquaintance with Bible prophecy and Jewish history, as to make a definite specification thereof unnecessary. Moreover, the context makes plain what it was that the election had obtained.

But let us, before proceeding further, observe that, whatever had been the object of Israel's quest, Israel had now (at the time the Epistle was written) *lost it irretrievably*; for the inspired utterance declares that, not only had Israel failed to obtain it, but another company, "the election," *had obtained it*. And furthermore, one of the chief purposes for which this passage (Romans IX-XI) was written was, to make known that God, in bestowing the coveted blessing upon the believing remnant of Israel and in incorporating with that remnant the saved from among the Gentiles, was *fulfilling the promises He had made by the mouth of His holy prophets to Israel*; "for they are not all 'Israel' which are of Israel" (9:6). Clearly then, what is here referred to is not something which that generation of Israelites had missed and God had temporarily withdrawn, with the intention of bestowing it upon a future generation.

And further let us observe preliminarily that Paul is not speaking here Of something that lay in the then future purposes of God, but of a promised blessing whereof the set time had come, a blessing which had in fact already passed into the possession of those for whom it had been intended, the People of God "*which He foreknew*" (v. 1). For the word is, "The election HATH obtained it.',

TO WHOM PERTAIN THE PROMISES

At the beginning of the Passage the apostle gives a list of seven things whereby God had distinguished the Israelites from all other Peoples (9:4, 5); which list includes "the promise." And there is no dispute, or room for it, that the blessings God had "promised Therefore by His prophets in the Holy Scriptures" were all expressly for "Israel," for "the seed of Abraham." Therefore, although the Jews of that day had misunderstood "the voices of the prophets" (Acts 13:27) and had carnalized the things their prophets had foretold, they were nevertheless not in error in the belief that the glorious things promised by them were all for "Israel." Their error, as has now been plainly pointed out in the N. T. Scriptures, was two-fold: *first* (as already shown) they misunderstood the *nature* of the promised blessings, for they supposed them to be natural and earthly, instead of spiritual and heavenly; and *second*, they did not understand that the promises were, not for the natural seed of Abraham, but for his spiritual seed; or in other words, that they who compose the true "Israel of God" are not those who have merely the outward "sign of circumcision," but those "who also walk in the steps of *that faith* of our father Abraham, which he had being yet uncircumcised" (Rom. 4:11, 12).

And so to-day, the differences that have arisen between those who study the prophetic Scriptures and seek the meaning thereof, are not as to whether the promises of God through the O. T. prophets were expressly for Israel, for the Jews, for the circumcision, for the seed of Abraham; but as to who *are* the "Israel" of promise? Who is "a Jew?" Who *are* "the circumcision?" and who "the seed of Abraham?" But how comes it that there are differences as to those questions between those who accept the New Testament as the Word of God? seeing that the first is expressly answered by Romans

9:6-8; the second by Romans 2:28, 29; the third by Philippians 3:3; and the fourth by Galatians 3:7, 29?

"THE PROMISE"

But at this point some will say: "True, there is a spiritual Israel as well as a natural Israel, an Israel of God' as well as an 'Israel after the flesh'; but may it not be that *some* of the blessings promised of old by the prophets of Israel are intended for the *natural* Israel, and are reserved for a yet future day? And is not the gift of the land of Canaan to Abraham and his seed a promise of that sort?

We believe a clear answer is to be found in the very passage we are now considering. For to begin with, if what Israel was then seeking after was the restoration of its nationality and there – possession of the land of Canaan – and undoubtedly that is what they were most ardently seeking – then manifestly the words, "the election hath obtained it," would be a complete bar to their hopes. But we look further into the matter.

The promises of God were numerous and were expressed in various ways; yet they were often viewed in their totality as a comprehensive whole. For example, in Galatians 3:7 we find the words, "heirs according to the promise"; as if all the promises scattered through the messages of the prophets constituted in the aggregate a single all-inclusive "promise," which in due time was to be fulfilled to "the seed of Abraham." Doubtless it is this comprehensive, all-embracing promise that Paul had in mind when he wrote of "that which he (Israel) seeketh for." And it is also quite certain, both from the Scriptures and also from Jewish history, that what that intensely patriotic people were ever seeking for was the repossession of the land of Canaan. And one of the Scriptures upon which their hopes were founded is this:

"For lo, the days come, saith the Lord, that I will bring again the captivity of my people Israel and Judah, saith the Lord; and I will cause them to return to the land that I gave to their fathers, and they shall possess it . . . "For it shall come to pass in that day, saith the Lord of hosts, that I will break his yoke from off thy neck, and shall burst thy bonds,

156

and strangers shall no more serve themselves to him; but they shall serve the Lord their God, and David their king, *whom I will raise up unto them*" (Jer. 30:3, 8, 9).

This is a typical expression of "the promise," and of what Israel was seeking after, according to their interpretation of it. Hence it is what they had failed to obtain, and *what the election had obtained.*

God's original promise to Abraham and his seed of a territorial possession is recorded in these words:

"And I will give unto thee, and unto thy seed after thee, the land wherein thou art a stranger, all the land of Canaan, for an everlasting possession" (Gen. 17:1-8).

Upon a close examination of this passage it will be seen that the promise is so worded that it would have been literally fulfilled had God thereafter given that land to the descendants of Ishmael; for Ishmael was as much the seed of Abraham as was Isaac. Later Scriptures, however, limit the promise to Isaac's descendants – "which things are an allegory" – and still later Scriptures limit it to the children of Jacob, excluding the off spring of Esau. But as between the twelve sons of Jacob no distinctions were made; and hence, if God should give that land to *any single descendant of Jacob*, it would be a *literal* fulfilment of the promise. And is not that precisely what God *has* done? But let us go a little further in quest of what the Scripture says concerning God's promise to Abraham.

In Romans 4, immediately following the verse quoted above, which tells who the real children of Abraham are, we read:

"For the promise that he should be *the heir of the world*, was not to Abraham or to his seed through the law, but through the righteousness of faith" (Rom. 4:13).

By this we learn that God's promise to Abraham was *much larger* than He chose to reveal in O. T. times. It embraced *the whole world*. And now that we know the full breadth of the promise, we clearly recognize that God, by giving the whole world to the seed of Abraham would *literally* fulfil this promise; for the greater includes the less.

The apostle then goes on to show that it is *impossible* that the promise to Abraham could be fulfilled to those who were merely his natural descendants: –

"For if they which are of the law be heirs, faith is made void, and *the promise made of none effect*" (Rom. 4:14).

In other words, the bestowal of the promised land upon the nation of Israel ("they which are of the law") would be –not *the fulfilling* of "the promise," but *the nullification* of it.

And the passage continues –

"Therefore it is of faith that it might be by grace, to the end *the promise might be sure to all* seed; not to that (seed) only which is of the law, but to that also which is of the faith of Abraham, who is the father of us all. (As it is written, I have made thee a father of many nations)".

By this we are given to know that the promise to Abraham, recorded in Genesis 17:1-8, runs to Abraham and his *spiritual* seed, those who are of the faith of Abraham, and that the clause "I have made thee a father of many nations" (Gen. 17:5), means that saved Gentiles were to be among the heirs of *this promise*.

The subject is still further elucidated in Galatians; where we read:

"Now to Abraham and his seed were the promises made. He saith not, And to seeds, as of many; but as of one, And to thy SEED, which is CHRIST (Gal. 3:16).

Thus we see that Christ is *the true and only legitimate Heir of the promise to Abraham*; but by the same Scripture (and by others as well) we learn that *Christ's members* are included with Him in the promise. In Galatians it is put thus:

"Even as Abraham believed God and it was counted to him for righteousness, know ye therefore, that they which are of faith, the same are *the children of Abraham*."

"And if ye be Christ's then are ye *Abraham's seed*, and heirs according to *the promise*" (Gal. 3:6, 7, 29).

Now, since "they which are of faith," they that are Christ's, are the elect remnant of Israel (with believing Gentiles incorporated

158

with them into one body) we have reached a clear explanation of what is meant by "the election hath obtained it." Christ and His people are the heirs "according to *the* promise," which embraces *all* the promises. It follows that there remains for the natural Israel nothing whatever of God's promise to Abraham concerning a territorial possession in the world. *The election hath obtained it*, and will never be dispossessed.

But, in order to put the matter beyond all doubt, the apostle not only states affirmatively who *are* the heirs of God's promise to Abraham, but he also shows negatively that Abraham's natural descendants have no share therein. He rebukes those of his contemporaries who held the contrary, charging them with not understanding the Scripture which records that "Abraham had *two* sons" (Gal. 4:21-31). We will not expatiate further on that wonderful "allegory"; but would merely remind the reader again that Ishmael represents Abraham's natural seed, and Isaac his spiritual seed, the latter being the heirs of the promise; and that the words, "cast out the bondwoman and her son, for the son of the bondwoman shall not be heir with the son of the freewoman," were a prophecy that the natural descendants of Abraham should not share the inheritance with his spiritual seed, the elect remnant.

Manifestly therefore, those who now maintain that the natural Israelites as such are the heirs of God's promise to Abraham, do not only fail to understand the allegorical significance of his family history, but they also close their eyes to the clear explanation thereof in Galatians 4:21-31.

In Romans 9:6-8 the same truth is stated in these words:

"For they are not all 'Israel,' which are *of* Israel. Neither because they are the seed of Abraham are they all *children*; but in Isaac shall thy seed be called. That is, They which are the children of the flesh, these are *not the children of God*: but the children of the Promise are counted for the seed."

This Scripture gives us, in addition to the important truth that not all Israelites are included in the "Israel" of God's prophetic purposes, the closely allied truth that "the children of God," that is,

159

those who are saved by the gospel, are "the children of *the* promise" (definite article in the original); and that they are *"counted for* the seed" (of Abraham). By this passage it is also seen that Romans IX continues a subject that was begun in Chapter VIII, *the inheritance of the whole redeemed creation by the children of God*. For in Chapter VIII it is written:

> "The Spirit Himself beareth witness with our spirit that we are *the children of God*: and if children, then heirs, heirs of God and joint-heirs with Christ") (Rom. 8:16, 17).

And the succeeding verses show that the inheritance here referred to is the entire creation of God, which is hereafter to be delivered from the bondage of corruption into the glorious liberty of the children of God.

Here is another Scripture which never could have been written if there were to be a Jewish millennium intervening between "the sufferings of this present time" and "the glory which shall be revealed in (or to) us" (v. 18).

HATH GOD CAST AWAY HIS PEOPLE?

If therefore, God had cast out the bondwoman and her son (Israel after the flesh) and had decreed that the son of the bondwoman was to have no share in the inheritance promised to Abraham ("the world"), could it be said that He had "cast away His people"? Manifestly if the natural descendants of Abraham were "His people," the answer would be, Yes. But Paul's answers to that question is an emphatic and indignant, "God forbid." And he goes on to explain that the natural Israelites were not His people; but that *"His people* which He foreknew" was that very small "remnant according to the election of grace" which believed in Jesus Christ (Rom. 11:1-7). The plain and decisive answer given by the apostle in this passage is, that God had not cast away *His people*, because the apostate nation which He had cast was not His people. Those were "the vessels of wrath *fitted to destruction*," which for centuries past He had "endured with much longsuffering" (Rom. 9:22), and to whom He had said through Isaiah, "All day long I have stretched

160

forth My hands unto *a disobedient and gainsaying people*" (10:20-21).

Those were not His people, and they *never were*, for when Elijah made intercession against "Israel," and instanced some of the enormities they had committed, what was God's answer? "I have *reserved to Myself* seven thousand men who have not bowed the knee to Baal." That "very small remnant" were all He owned as His people in that day; and Paul says, "EVEN SO" it is "at this present time also"; and he had shown in the preceding chapter (9:25, 26) that "this present time" is the "that day" foretold of God through Hosea, in which He would disown His nominal people as "*not* My people," and would "call them *My people* which were not My people" (Hos. 1:9; 2:23). There is no obscurity in the apostle's answer to his own question, "Hath God cast away His people?" the answer being in effect that God had in contemplation a people, "which He *foreknew*," which were not the natural Israel (for only a small fraction of that nation were to be included among them) and these He had not cast away, but on the contrary they had obtained and were already in possession of that which the natural Israel had been vainly seeking for.

And yet, in the interest of modern Dispensationalism, this luminous explanation is not merely disregarded, but is *reversed*; and the passage is made to mean that the *natural Israelites* are God's people, and that as such they are to "obtain" in a future dispensation that which they have been seeking for.

THE KINGDOM OF GOD

What Israel was seeking for was usually in those days designated by the then current expressions, "Kingdom of God" and "Kingdom of the heavens"; and the Holy Spirit has made use of those terms in the New Testament. Therefore, in closing this chapter, it is appropriate to call attention to the fact that, what Paul was inspired to reveal in detail in Romans and Galatians, had been briefly foretold by the Lord Himself in His last words spoken to chief priests and elders of the people just before His death. It is recorded by Matthew that, after speaking to those Jewish leaders the parable

161

of the Wicked Husbandmen, the Lord put to them a question which led them to pronounce the doom of their nation. For, replying to His question – "What will he [the lord of the vineyard] do to those wicked husbandman?" –they said:

> "He will miserably destroy those wicked men, and will let out his vineyard to other husbandman, which shall render him the fruits in their season" (Mat. 21:33-41).

Little did they imagine that, in so speaking, they were uttering a true prophecy of what was about to happen to that nation.   But the next words of Jesus make this clear; for He said:

> "Therefore I say unto you, The Kingdom of God shall be *taken from you*, and given to *a nation* bringing forth the fruits thereof" (v. 43).

What Christ declares in these words is the same thing in substance as what Paul afterwards stated, when he said: "Israel hath not obtained that which he seeketh for, but the election hath obtained it"; for obviously, "the election" is that "nation" to which, according to the words of Christ, the kingdom of God (which Israel was seeking for) was to be given. The election is that "holy nation," which "in time past were not a people, but now are the people of God" (I Pet. 2:9).

Further discussion of the subject of *the people of God*, and particularly of the place which Gentiles have in that company, will be found in the next succeeding chapter.

THE WORD OF FAITH WHICH WE PREACH

A specific instance of that which Israel was seeking for and had not obtained, but which the believing remnant had obtained, is found in the reference which Paul makes in Romans 10 to the last prophecy of Moses concerning Israel. That citation is of the highest importance; for it furnishes in and of itself conclusive proof that the promises of future mercy to Israel, when they should repent and return to the Lord, are promises of *gospel-salvation*, not of *national restoration*. Therefore we ask special attention to what follows:

162

Immediately preceding the words quoted by Paul from Deuteronomy 30, are prophecies of the complete apostasy of Israel; foretellings of the days to come when they would turn from the Lord, would break His covenant and serve other gods, even sacrificing unto devils; because of which He would bring upon them all the curses written in the book of the law, *"until He have destroyed thee"* (Deut. 28:45, 48, 61; and 29: 24-28).

But now, against the background of that dark cloud of coming judgment, God sets the lustrous bow of promised mercy. Let us therefore pay careful attention to the words of Moses and to the explanation of them the Spirit has given through the apostle Paul:

"And it shall come to pass, when all these things are come upon thee ... and thou shalt call them to mind among all the nations whither the Lord thy God hath driven thee, and shalt *return unto the Lord thy God,* and shalt obey His voice, according to all that I command thee this day, thou and thy children, with all thy heart and with all thy soul; that then the Lord thy God will *turn thy captivity.* and have compassion on thee, and *will return and gather thee from all the nations whither the Lord thy God hath scattered thee* ...

"And the Lord thy God will bring thee into the land thy fathers possessed, and thou shalt possess it . . . And the Lord will *circumcise thine heart,* and the heart of all thy seed, to love the Lord thy God with all thine heart and with all thy soul, that thou mayest live .... And thou shalt return and obey the voice of the Lord, and do all His commandments which I command thee this day." (Deut. 30:1-8).

Here we have a clear statement of what Israel was seeking for; and we can readily understand how the unspiritual rabbis, those "blind leaders of the blind," should have interpreted this and similar scriptures as promises of political restoration for Israel and of the repossession by that nation of the earthly Canaan; for they were blinded to the truth that the land of Canaan was but a fleeting "shadow" (Heb. 10:1) of the true land of promise (Eph. 1:3); even as

163

the earthly nation itself was but the shadow "for the time then present," of the true Israel of God.

And then follow these words, to which we specially invite attention:

"For this commandment, which I command thee this day, it is not hidden from thee, neither is it far off . It is not in heaven, that thou shouldest say, Who shall go up for us to heaven, and bring it unto us, that we may hear it and do it? Neither is it beyond the sea, that thou shouldest say, Who shall go over the sea for us, and bring it unto us, that we may hear it and do it? But the word is very nigh unto thee, in thy mouth and in thy heart, that thou mayest do it" (Deut. 30:11-14).

Paul quotes from this scripture and says that Moses was referring there to *"the word of faith which we preach,"* that is, the gospel; and he declares the inner meaning of these words of Moses to be, "That if thou shalt confess *with thy mouth* the Lord Jesus" – Moses had said *"in thy mouth* and *in thy heart"* – "and shalt believe *in thine heart* that God hath raised him from the dead, thou shalt be *saved"* (Rom. 10:9). And the apostle goes on to say that the promise was not for penitent Jews only, but for all men: "For there is no difference between the Jew and the Greek; for *whosoever* shall call on the name of the Lord shall be saved" (vv. 12, 13).

The essence of all this, stated in the fewest words, is that "this commandment which" – Moses said – "I command thee this day," and which was to be brought "very nigh" unto them, was *to hear and obey the gospel of Christ.*

And from this Paul argues the imperative necessity of preaching the gospel to all men, *Jews and Gentiles alike;* "for how shall they believe in Him of whom they have not heard? and how shall they hear without a preacher?" And, still keeping Moses' prophecy in view, he continues:

"But – I say, Did not Israel know? [that God's promised mercy was to embrace Gentiles also]. First Moses saith, I will provoke you to jealousy by them that are no People, and by a foolish nation I will anger You. But Esaias is very bold, and saith, I was found of them that sought me not; I was made manifest unto them that asked not after me. But to Israel he saith, All day long I have stretched forth my hands unto a disobedient and gainsaying people." (Rom. 10:18-21).

And then the apostle sums up the truth of the matter by saying: "Israel hath not obtained that which he seeketh for; but the election hath obtained it, and the rest were blinded."

Here we have an authoritative explanation of God's promise of mercy for some future generation of Israelites upon condition of repentance and faith; and thereby we learn that, although it spoke of things seemingly material and earthly, such as the re-possession of the tiny bit of earth's surface formerly possessed by their ancestors, it was in reality a promise of *gospel-salvation*. Further we learn thereby that the promise is being fulfilled *now* to all those Jews (the remnant according to the election of grace) who confess the crucified Jesus as LORD and who believe in their heart that God has raised Him from the dead; and that the promise is for believing Gentiles as well as for believing Jews.

By this explanation we learn also that the failure of Israel as a nation to obtain the promise of Deuteronomy XXX, which the remnant has obtained, is in fulfilment not only of the prophecies of Moses but of other prophecies as well; such for example as that which God spake through Isaiah, saying: "All day long I have stretched forth My hands unto a disobedient and gainsaying people." Both classes of prophecies – blessings and cursings – are in course of fulfilment *now*. For it necessarily follows that all similar prophecies of mercy and restoration for the Jewish people are prophecies of gospel salvation, and have their fulfilment in this present day of grace. And it is appropriate at this point to recall once more the enlightening word spoken by Peter, whereby we know that it was revealed to Israel's prophets that the things foretold by them they ministered, "not unto themselves, but unto us"; which prophecies are the very things now reported by those that have preached the gospel unto us with the Holy Ghost sent down from heaven. (1 P. 1: 10-12).

CHAPTER XVIII

BUILDING AGAIN THE TABERNACLE OF DAVID

The apostle James, in announcing the decision of the great and epoch-making Conference of the apostles and elders at Jerusalem (Acts 15:1-21) which Conference was historically the first General Council of the Christian Church, cited the words of the prophet Amos, through whom God had said: *"In that day will I raise up again the tabernacle of David, that is fallen"* (Amos 9:11).

The present writer has frequently been asked the meaning of this prophecy concerning the tabernacle of David; and inasmuch as the passage is sometimes referred to in support of the idea of a future restoration of the Jewish nation, it is appropriate that due consideration be given to it in this volume.

By reference to Acts 15:1-21, it will be seen that the question presented for the decision of the Conference was whether the Gentiles, who had been converted to Christ, should be circumcised and commanded to keep the law of Moses (v. 5). For some had taught them, saying, "Except ye be circumcised after the manner of Moses, ye cannot be saved" (v. 1). That question was of capital importance, as may be clearly seen in the light of Paul's Epistle to the churches of Galatia. The conference, therefore, marked a momentous epoch in the history of the Kingdom of God.

For a proper understanding of this record, and particularly the words of James, we must give heed to the fact that the Jerusalem conference had to do wholly and solely with *"the conversion of the Gentiles"* (v. 3), which was not only a new thing, but to the Jewish disciples was a most astonishing thing, a thing for which they were, in fact, wholly unprepared.

Peter was the first to speak. He related how God had instructed him to go to the house of Cornelius, where a company of *Gentiles* was awaiting him, and what had taken place there. Then Barnabas and Paul addressed the conference, "declaring what miracles and wonders God had wrought among *the Gentiles* by them" (v. 12). And finally James addressed the assemblage, saying:

"Simeon hath declared how God at the first (i. e. for the first time) did visit *the Gentiles*, to take out *of them* a people for His name. And *to this* agree the words of the prophets; as it is written, After this I will return, and *will build again the tabernacle of David*, which is fallen down; and I will build again the ruins thereof, and will set it up: That the residue of men might seek after the Lord, and *all the Gentiles upon whom My Name is called*, saith the Lord, who doeth all these things. Known unto God are all His works from the beginning of the world" (vv. 14:18).

According to the writer's understanding of the passage, the era contemplated by the words, "After this I will return," is *this present Gospel dispensation*, whereof the conversion of Gentiles is the conspicuous feature (the "mystery," Eph. 3:3-6); and that "the tabernacle of David" is a prophetic symbol of that "spiritual house," into which converted Gentiles, along with converted Jews, "as living stones," are being builded together, upon Christ, the "sure Foundation," "for an habitation of God through the Spirit" (Matt. 16:18; Eph. 2:20-22; 1 Pet. 2:5, 6; Isa. 28: 16).

From James' words alone it is clear that God's promise through the prophet Amos, that He would "build again the tabernacle of David," was related to what He was just then beginning to do, namely, visiting *the Gentiles*, to take out from among them a people for His Name. For, after rehearsing what Simon Peter had just told them, how that God had chosen that apostle as the instrument whereby He, for the first time, "did visit" a company of Gentiles for the Purpose stated above, James plainly declared that *to this* (God's visitation of the Gentiles to take out of them a people for His Name) agreed the words of the prophets (in general), and those of Amos (in the passage quoted) in particular.

This connects the promise concerning the building again of the tabernacle of David directly with God's work, then just commenced, of converting sinners from among the Gentiles. It fixes beyond all question the time of the building again of the tabernacle of David; for it definitely locates that promised work in this gospel era, during all of which God has been visiting and converting the Gentiles. And when we connect with this the further fact, clearly stated in the N.

T., that God's chief purpose in converting sinners of the Gentiles is that He may use them as "living stones," in the building of that "spiritual house" which He is now raising up, our way to a right understanding of the passage seems fairly clear. For it only remains to inquire whether we are warranted by the Word of God in taking "the tabernacle of David," spoken of by Amos, as a prophetic symbol of that "habitation of God," which is now being "built upon the foundation of the apostles and prophets, Jesus Christ Himself being the chief Corner Stone" (Eph. 2:20-22).

"AFTER THIS"

Let it then be kept in mind, as we proceed with our inquiry, that the great Jerusalem Conference was occupied – not with some *future* work of God, but – with what He had *at that very time* begun to do. For His visitation of the Gentiles, beginning through Peter at the house of Cornelius and continuing through Paul and Barnabas in various places in Asia Minor, was the subject, *and the only subject*, so far as the record discloses, that was considered at that Conference. In view of this fact, and of other considerations hereafter noted, it is clear that the words, "after this," do not specify a period of time subsequent to this present gospel dispensation (as supposed by some), but a period subsequent to the time when Amos spoke his prophecy. For James is giving, in verses 15-17, not a prophecy of his own, but that of Amos; and he is stating, moreover, the substance of other O. T. prophecies. When James declared that the words of the prophets "agreed" with what Peter had just related concerning his mission to the house of Cornelius, he used a word which means literally to "sound together, to *symphonize*," as when the instruments of an orchestra play in perfect harmony. Thus we are given clearly to know that the reports which Peter, Paul and Barnabas had brought to that Conference, concerning God's wonderful work in visiting and saving numbers of Gentiles, is just what had been foretold by the prophets in general (see Rom. 15:8-12), and particularly by Amos, whose words James proceeds to quote. This makes it certain that the phrase "after this" refers to some period subsequent to the days of the O. T. prophets, and not to a period yet future. In fact it is entirely clear from the whole record of the Conference, that James applied "the words of the prophets," including the phrase "after this," to what God was then doing in visiting the Gentiles.

Furthermore, the exact words which God spake by the prophet Amos were, "*In that day*" (not "after this") "I will raise up the tabernacle of David that is fallen" etc. (Am. 9:11); and the Holy Spirit, speaking by James, gives us to understand that the words, "after this," correctly express what Amos meant by "in that day"; and that they express also what was meant by other prophets, who had foretold the salvation of the Gentiles. Now the two preceding verses of Amos make it plain that the "day" whereof he was speaking is *this present era*; for it is now that the Israelites are "sifted from among all the nations (v. 9).

Hence the Scriptures thus far considered compel us to look for some work of God *in this present age* as the fulfilment of the prophecy that He would "raise up the tabernacle of David"; and for a work that involves the conversion of the Gentiles.

This brings us to the question, What then is ...

THE TABERNACLE OF DAVID?

To begin with, let us note that it is not the temple of Solomon. The two structures were quite distinct; and typically they differ widely in significance. Amos prophesied concerning a "tabernacle," definitely associated with *David*, a tabernacle which, at the time of his prophecy, had "fallen," and was in "ruins." Amos prophesied "in the days of Uzziah, king of Judah" (1:1), at which time the temple of Solomon was standing in all its glory, and its services and sacrifices were being carried out in due order. There is doubtless something very significant in the fact that, while the temple of Solomon was yet standing, God declared His purpose to raise up *the tabernacle of David* that is *fallen*," and to "raise up its *ruins*."

Historically, the tabernacle of David was the tent wherein the ark of God was housed during the latter part of David's reign. In 2 Samuel Chapter 6 is the account of the bringing up of the ark of God "into the city of David with gladness" (v. 12); and it is recorded that "they brought the ark of the Lord, and set it in its place, in the midst *of the tabernacle* that *David* had pitched for it" (v. 17). Thus "the tabernacle of David," pitched in "Zion," the city of David, became *the dwelling place of Jehovah*; and hence it is most natural and fitting that it should become in prophecy the figure or symbol of that "tabernacle of God," which the Son of David was to build, according to the true meaning and intent of the word of the Lord by Nathan, recorded in the very next chapter of 2 Samuel: "He shall build *an house for My Name*, and I will establish the throne of his kingdom forever" (2 Sam. 7:13).[1] This conclusion finds strong support in the fact that the name of David's city, *Zion*, is used in many prophecies, and also in the New Testament, as the designation of *God's eternal habitation*.

Recurring to the prophecy of Amos, it will be clearly seen that his statements could not be taken as applying to the literal tent that David had set up to receive the ark. Even if that frail structure had survived, in a condition of dilapidation, to the days of Amos, still the terms "breaches" and "ruins," used by Amos, and the phrase "build again" of James, would be inapplicable to a mere tent. Nor would it require a work of *God* to raise it up and repair it. So we are driven to the conclusion that the raising again of the tabernacle of David, spoken of by the prophet, was the figure of a work which *God Himself* would undertake to accomplish; a work that was of great importance in His eyes, and that would require for its accomplishment the putting forth of His mighty quickening power. And such indeed is the building of that "spiritual house" whereof "Jesus Christ of the seed of David, risen from the dead" (2 Tim. 2:7), is the true foundation, the tried Corner Stone laid "in Zion"; and upon which converted Jews and Gentiles having been "quickened together with Christ," are "as living stones," being built up, "to offer spiritual sacrifices acceptable to God by Jesus Christ" (1 Pet. 2:4-6). In this view of the prophecy it does indeed "agree" with what God was beginning to do in the days of the Jerusalem conference, as reported by the apostles, Peter, Paul and Barnabas.

---

[1] It should be noted that the words, "for My name," link this promise with the words of James, "to take out of them a people *for His Name*."

170

AS LIVING STONES

Peter, who was the first speaker in that Conference, gives clear light, in his first Epistle, upon the matter which was there under deliberation, and which is also the subject of our present inquiry. For the revelation of truth given in that Epistle culminates in the statement of chapter 11, that those whom God has begotten again unto a living hope by the resurrection of Jesus Christ from the dead, who have been redeemed with His precious blood, as of a lamb without blemish and without spot, and have been born again of the incorruptible seed of the word of God, as declared in Chapter 1, are, as "living stones," being built up a spiritual house, upon Jesus Christ, the "living Stone" which the builders rejected, made in resurrection "the head of the corner." And the apostle quotes in this connection Isaiah 28:16, "Wherefore also it is contained in the Scripture, Behold, I lay *in Zion* a chief corner stone, elect, precious; and he that believeth on Him shall not be confounded."

This citation from Isaiah establishes two facts of capital importance; *first*, that God's eternal habitation is being built, not in the natural world, but in the spiritual world; and *second*, that the "Zion" of prophecy, which God has chosen as the place of His eternal abode, is the *heavenly* Zion, to which we "are come" (Heb. 12:22). These two facts constitute strong evidence confirmatory of the correctness of our explanation of Acts 15:16. For the tabernacle that David built for the ark was *in Zion*, the city of David; and inasmuch as the name "Zion" designates a *spiritual locality*, the place of God's eternal dwelling, it would naturally follow that the expression "tabernacle of David" has also a *spiritual* meaning. Furthermore, when God, by the lips of His prophet, declares that He Himself will, in a certain specified era, raise up again that which had formerly been His temporary dwelling place, and when, in that very era, we learn from His servants, Peter and Paul, that He is actually building for Himself an *eternal dwelling place*, the conclusion is well nigh irresistible that the building He is now raising up is the one He said He would raise up in this present dispensation.

AN HABITATION OF GOD

In complete agreement with this revelation by Peter, is what Paul wrote in his Epistle to the Ephesians, concerning that masterpiece of God's "workmanship" which He is raising up at the present time, that wondrous building, "fitly framed together," built "upon the foundation of the apostles and prophets, Jesus Christ Himself being the chief corner stone, for an habitation of God through the Spirit" (Eph. 2:10, 20) But Paul goes more fully into the subject, and he clearly identifies this great building with what had been under consideration at the Jerusalem Conference, by emphasizing the place which the saved from among the Gentiles have in this great work of God. That equal participation of saved Gentiles with saved Jews in the *one* "household of God") (Eph. 2:11-19) is "*the mystery of Christ*, which," writes this apostle, "in other ages was not made known unto the sons of men, as it is now revealed unto His holy apostles and prophets by the Spirit"; and that mystery was, as the apostle himself defines it: "That the Gentiles should be *fellow heirs*, and of the *same* body, and partakers of His promise in Christ, by the gospel" (Eph. 3:4-6).

OTHER DETAILS OF THE PASSAGE

It has been already pointed out that the words "which is fallen down" &c. could not be taken as applying either to the literal tent which David had erected as a habitation for the ark, or to Solomon's temple. In what sense then was the tabernacle of David is fallen down and in ruins? To find an explanation for those words we must needs take them in a *figurative* sense; and there should be no hesitation or reluctance so to do, seeing that figurative language is the customary language of the prophets. And a most satisfactory explanation of those expressions immediately presents itself, when we call to mind that *God's people* constitute His true dwelling place. It was Israel that was "fallen," and that was, in God's contemplation, in "ruins." It was Israel that God purposed to "raise up again" – not, of course, the natural Israel, but the spiritual Israel, the true "Israel of God," a people composed of the saved remnant of the natural Israel, with whom are incorporated into one body, forming one spiritual house, the called from among the Gentiles. To these Amos

172

refs in the words "remnant of Edom, and of all the heathen (Gentiles) upon whom My Name is called (Am. 9:12, *marg*.). Instead of "remnant of *Edom*" James has "residue of *men*," which indicates that Amos used the word "Edom" figuratively to designate all who were not "Jacob," that is, non-Israelites.

The words "Gentiles upon whom *My Name* is called" refer back to the words "to take out of them a people for *His Name*"; which further serves to show that the prophecy of Amos has its fulfilment in God's present day visitation of the Gentiles.

The word "tabernacle" is used of God's dwelling place in the N. T. Thus we read in Hebrews 8:1, 2 concerning Christ that He is "a minister of the sanctuary, and of the *true tabernacle* which the Lord pitched, and not man"; and again, in the last vision of the Apocalypse, John saw the New Jerusalem coming down from heaven, and heard a great voice saying, "Behold, *the tabernacle of God* is with men" (Rev. 21:1-3). Moreover, in this connection the Lord Jesus announces Himself as "The Root and Offspring of David" (22:16).

In the prophecy of Amos we have the words of God, "And I will build it, *as in the days of old*." The days when David pitched a tabernacle in Zion for the ark were days of joy and gladness, of shouting and dancing, of victory and prosperity, the days when David reigned over a united and a happy people. It is recorded that "He blessed the people in the Name of the Lord of hosts. And he dealt among all the people, even among the whole multitude of Israel, as well to the women as men, to every one a cake of bread, and a good piece of flesh, and a flagon of wine" (2 Sam. 6:12-19). It is not difficult to see in this description a type of those eternal joys which all will share together, when at last "*the tabernacle of God* shall be with men, and He will dwell with them, and they shall be His people; and God Himself shall be with them and be their God."

GEORGE SMITH ON THE TABERNACLE OF DAVID

Very little seems to have been written on the subject of the Tabernacle of David; therefore the writer was glad to find, in

173

George Smith's *Harmony of the Divine Dispensations* (published in 1856) some illuminating comments thereon.

The chapter is much too long to be reproduced here in full. But some extracts are given below, prefaced by a brief explanation of what precedes the quoted paragraphs.

Mr. Smith wonders that there should ever have been any uncertainty as to what was meant in the prophecies of Isaiah 16:5 and Amos 9:11 by "the tabernacle of David"; seeing that the Scriptures give such great prominence to "*the tabernacle* that David had pitched" for the ark of the covenant. One account of the removal of the ark to the tabernacle that David prepared for it on Mount Zion is given in 2 Samuel 6:5,7; and again in 1 Chronicles 16:1 it is recorded that "they brought the ark of God, and set it in the midst of *the tent that David had pitched for it.*" Moreover both accounts make evident that the housing of the ark of God in the tabernacle of David was an event of unusual importance; for it was celebrated by "all Israel" with demonstrations of the most impressive character – "with shouting, and with sound of the cornet, and with trumpets and with cymbals," while King David himself danced before the ark with all his might in the exuberance of his joy. And then followed sacrifices of burnt offerings and peace offerings, and the distribution "to every one of Israel, both man and woman," of the king's bounty, flesh, bread and wine for a feast. And furthermore the event was signalized by the fact that "Then on that day David delivered first this Psalm to thank the Lord into the hand of Asaph and his brethren" (that is, Psalm 105 and parts of other Psalms: see 2 Sam. 23:1, and 1 Chron. 16:7).

But, as Mr. Smith points out, the most remarkable and significant feature of this great historical event is that it constituted a decided break with the levitical ordinances given through Moses, *in that the ark of God's presence was no longer in the holy of holies of the Tabernacle of the Wilderness* (which was then at Gibeon), but in the midst of the Tabernacle of David on Mount Zion; and further that there were *no animal sacrifices there*, only sacrifices of praise and thanksgiving; and *no priests*, but only *Levites*, whom David appointed "to minister before the ark of the Lord, and to record," that is literally to *make mention of*, or *bring to remembrance*, or in other words to proclaim or preach the mercies and the marvelous acts of God, "and to thank and praise the Lord God of Israel" (1 Chr. 16:4). This was a very remarkable suspension of the system of worship of the Law, and an equally remarkable foreshadowing of that of the Gospel. And so it was during the greater part of King David's reign, during all the years the ark of God dwelt in the Tabernacle of David.

Chiefly it is to be observed that this sojourn of the ark on Mount Zion is the foundation of the many references in the Psalms and the Prophets to *Zion, as the dwelling place of Jehovah*, and is what gives to the terms "Zion" and "Mount Zion" their high spiritual meaning. And it is a most significant fact, whereof we must take due notice if we are to understand some of the most important of the prophecies, that *never thereafter* was Mount Moriah, where Solomon's magnificent temple stood, referred to as Jehovah's dwelling place, but always Mount Zion; and that when God speaks by His prophets concerning things to come in the Kingdom of Christ, He never says "I will build again the Temple of Solomon which I destroyed," but "I will build again the Tabernacle of David which is fallen down."

Thus, the Tabernacle of David is evidently replete with typical meaning, concerning which it will suffice for our present purpose to remark that, to David, the man after God's own heart, who was himself a conspicuous type of Christ, and who is more closely associated with the gospel than any other of the patriarchs (Mat. 1:1; Ac. 13:22, 34; Ro. 1:3; 2 Tim. 2:8;Rev. 27:16, etc.) it was given to know the mind of God concerning real spiritual worship; and that he, "being a prophet, and knowing that God had sworn with an oath to him, that of the fruit of his loins according to the flesh, He would *raise up* Christ to sit on his throne" (Ac. 2:30) was permitted to give in the tabernacle pitched by him on Mount Zion, a wonderful foreshadowing of the worship, by prayer, preaching and song, which characterizes the gatherings of God's people in this gospel dispensation.

The spiritual worship thus begun was not continued in the reign of subsequent Kings; for a fearful decline began in the days of Solomon and continued to the end of the kingdom era. But Amos, in the days of Uzziah, delivered that famous prophecy concerning the raising up of the Tabernacle of David (Am. 9:11, 12), which all the apostles, elders and people assembled at Jerusalem accepted as decisive of the question whether the Mosaic ritual was to be imposed upon Gentile converts (Ac. 15:417). Citing the words of Amos, Mr. Smith says it was –

"A prophecy which clearly places before us the genius and character, religious services and spirit of *the tabernacle of David*, as similar and precursor to the, Kingdom of Christ." And then, after quoting Isaiah's prophecy (16:5) concerning "the Tabernacle of David," he continues:

> "These prophecies considerably enlarge our field of vision with respect to the relation of the tabernacle of David to the kingdom of Christ. According to these, the Shekinah, resting over the cherubim in the sanctuary of Mount Zion, typified the reign of Christ in the Gospel Church. In fact this is the true line of descent, and the true exposition of the kingdom of Christ. For here, in those gracious institutions of a remembered and proclaimed covenant mercy, and those thanksgivings of grateful love (poured out in songs of praise), Messiah sits ruling in the hearts of His people, dispensing truth, and hastening them on to the attainment of righteousness."

Referring to the question brought up for decision at Jerusalem, whereof an account is given in Acts 15, Mr. Smith says:

> "The decision of that question, so vitally important to the rising Church, was formally referred to the apostles and elders at Jerusalem. Paul, Barnabas and others went from Antioch to the Hebrew capital to take part in this important discussion. Peter, Barnabas and Paul recited the wonders wrought among the Gentiles by the preaching of the Gospel. But still there was wanting some *clear, pointed, powerful, Scriptural authority* to effect the permanent settlement of a question of such magnitude. And it was supplied by James, who quoted the words of the text (Amos 9:10, 11) as incontrovertible evidence on the case. The question was, *Must the ritual law of Moses be obeyed by*

Christian converts? To this the apostle replied, 'Certainly not; for inspired prophecy declares that the kingdom of Christ is not to be a revival and extension of Mosaicism, but on the contrary a restoration of the tabernacle of David. And since in that sanctuary the Mosaic ritual had no place, so it can have no claims in the Christian Church? The most important feature of this case is the *perfect unanimity* with which this judgment was received and adopted. This was a meeting composed almost entirely of Hebrews, whose sympathies and prejudices inclined them to the observance of the ordinances of the law. Yet no sooner is the citation of sacred Prophecy made, than all perceive its force, all admit its decisive effect. Even the great body of believers unanimously concur. And there *in Jerusalem itself, within sight of the temple, where the ritual of the law was still performed in all its extent and minuteness*, the whole body of the Church repudiate its claims, and adopt *the Tabernacle of David* as the Divinely appointed model for all Christian practice and institutions."

As to the effects: The first effect of the decision was to sweep away forever the assertion, "Except ye be circumcised, ye cannot be saved." For, says our author,

"Circumcision fell and perished from the Christian Church before the Divinely inspired quotation of the prophecy of Amos by the apostle James. Sacrifice was abolished with circumcision. For that institution formed no part of the worship offered to God on Mount Zion.

"With circumcision and sacrifice the priesthood was also abolished. Indeed an unsacrificing priesthood is a contradiction of terms; for every priest is 'ordained to offer gifts and sacrifices' (Heb. 8:3). But there was nothing of that kind in the tabernacle of David, whose sacred services therefore vividly represented the worship proper to that church which is redeemed by the blood of the Lamb, Whose 'one sacrifice for sins' is universally and everlastingly efficacious –'once for all' (Heb. 10:10). Nor must it be forgotten that, with those elements of the Mosaic economy, every existing *typical* and *symbolical* thing was swept away" (That is to say *all* the shadows" of the law, were abolished and replaced by the corresponding spiritual realities). "It is astonishing that educated Christian men should evince so much weakness and ignorance as have been of late displayed; not to use stronger terms."

"The tabernacle of David evidently arose from the existence and felt wants of men. They needed means of more direct union with God and communion with His Spirit, than was afforded by priestly instrumentality in the national sanctuary. And it pleased God to sanction and honor such a deviation from His own appointed ordinances as would meet that need. Hence the Ark of God and His glory dwelt in the sanctuary of Zion. There the people met before the Lord. There they heard the wonders of His covenant mercy and felt the power of His saving grace. How marvelous are the merciful manifestations of God! Who would have supposed that the Mosaic system could, in one great feature of its operation, have been suspended for so many years? That this measure should have been wrought up into sacred prophecy, and used under apostolic inspiration to cast a steady light on the true character of the Gospel Church, and to show the nature of Gospel institutions? Yet so it is. And so fully is this the case that none can adequately apprehend the glorious development of grace which has attended the revelation of the Gospel, without a recognition of the Tabernacle of David, and some acquaintance with its services and its position in prophecy.

"How beautiful is the harmony with which these views put before us the merciful revelation of Divine grace to mankind! The law was introduced as a mighty persuasive and protest against idolatry, and for the purpose of setting forth, by the most significant and vivid typical action, the redeeming work of the Lord Jesus. This being done, the Tabernacle of David is raised, and Mount Zion becomes the seat of a manifestation of spiritual privilege and saving grace, which, in a great measure, anticipated the blessings of the Gospel, and was exactly adapted to prepare the world, and especially the Hebrew church, for the coming and Kingdom of God's Messiah."

The foregoing quotations present what impresses the writer as being a sound, sane, satisfying and above all, *Scriptural*, exposition of the Word of truth!

CALVIN'S COMMENT ON MICAH 4.6.

In connection with the subject of the building of the tabernacle of David, Calvin's comment on a parallel prophecy is worthy of special consideration.

Micah 4:6, 7 reads: –

"6. In that day, saith the Lord, will I assemble her that halteth, and I will gather her that I have afflicted:

"7. And I will make her that halted a remnant, and her that was cast off a strong nation; and the Lord shall reign over them in Mount Zion from henceforth even forever."

Commenting on verse 6, Calvin (as quoted in Karl Barth's great book on The Word of God) says:

"Although the Church is at the present time hardly to be distinguished from a dead, or at best a sick, man, there is no reason for despair; for the Lord raises up His own *suddenly*, as He waked the dead from the grave. This we must clearly remember lest, when the Church fails to shine forth, we conclude too quickly that her light has died utterly away. But the Church in the world is so preserved that she rises suddenly from the dead. Her very preservation through the years is due to a succession of such miracles. Let us cling to the remembrance that she is not without her resurrection, or rather, not without her many resurrections."

For it is to be remembered that, as already pointed out, the true Israel is a resurrection from the putrid carcass of the natural Israel.

As regards verse 7, we have a record of the fulfilment thereof in 1 Pet. 2:9, where we read of a remnant that had been made a nation.

At verse 10 the prophet foretells the birth-pangs of the daughter of Zion in the bringing forth of this "nation"; and a few verses further on (5:1) he speaks of the treatment the Judge of Israel was to receive at the hands of that people, and which was to precipitate that travail.

CHAPTER XIX
SHALL ISRAEL BE RESTORED AS A NATION?

Under the above title a writer, in a recent issue of a religious periodical, undertakes to give scriptural evidence in support of the doctrine that the natural seed of Jacob are hereafter to be reconstituted as an earthly nation, and as such are to reoccupy the land of Canaan.

This attempt is commendable. For it is surely incumbent upon those who uphold the doctrine above referred to, to bring clear proof thereof from the Word of God. Moreover, it will help the reader to form his own independent judgment on the important matter we are considering, if we call his attention to the passages of Scripture relied upon by those who hold the doctrine of the national restoration of Israel.

What evidences then does this writer advance?

First he quotes Jeremiah 31:35-37; and to this passage particular heed should be given; for of course the first witness will be one upon whose testimony special reliance is placed. Here is the passage:

"Thus saith the Lord that giveth the sun for a light by day, and the ordinances of the moon and of the stars for a light by night, that divideth the sea when the waves thereof roar; the LORD of hosts is His name: If those ordinances depart from before Me, then the seed of Israel shall cease from being a nation before Me forever. Thus saith the Lord; If heaven above can be measured, and the foundations of the earth searched out beneath, I will also cast off all the seed of Israel for all that they have done, saith the Lord."

Do these verses declare that the earthly Israel are hereafter to be restored nationally?

Looking at the context, which is the way to learn what is the subject of the prophecy, we find that the verses quoted above follow immediately God's promise of the "new covenant," which (He says)

181

was to be "not according to the covenant that I made with their fathers in the day that I took them by the hand to bring them out of the land of Egypt, *which My covenant they brake.*" Under that old covenant earthly blessings were promised to an earthly people, including national existence and the possession of the land of Canaan. Those blessings, moreover (and it is important to observe this) were made to depend upon express conditions, to be faithfully observed by that people, and were to be forfeited if those conditions were not observed. But that covenant, the Lord declares, "they brake." And now, through Jeremiah, He proclaims the great fact that He will make, in a time then future, "a new covenant," which was to be of *a different sort.*

The Epistle to the Hebrews explains fully this prophecy of Jeremiah concerning the new covenant, the prophecy itself being quoted in full in Heb. 8:7-13, and in part in 10:15-17. It is the "everlasting covenant," secured by the blood of Jesus Christ (Heb. 13: 20). It is established with a heavenly people, those who are "come to Mount Sion, and to the city of the living God the *heavenly* Jerusalem, . . . and to the church of the first born (ones) who are written (i.e. enrolled) *in heaven*" (Ch. 12:22, 23). It is "a better covenant established upon better promises" (Ch. 8:6). It is the covenant whereunder every repentant and believing sinner, whether Jew or Gentile, receives the forgiveness of his sins (Ch. 10:12-18). And finally, it is the *only* covenant under which God henceforth deals with any part of the human family; for Hebrews gives great prominence to the truth that *the old covenant,* with its conditional promises of national prosperity and an earthly country (promises long since forfeited by rebellion and apostasy) *has been set aside completely and forever* (8:13, 10:9).

Furthermore, our Lord Himself fixed the interpretation of this prophecy of Jeremiah, and showed that it has its fulfilment in *Himself and His redeemed people* ("the Israel of God"), when, in instituting His memorial supper, He said, "This is My blood of *the new covenant,* shed for many for the remission of sins" (Mat. 26:28).

Beyond all question therefore, the prophecy we are considering pertains to *this present gospel era* (not to some future day); and it has its consummation in that "holy nation" (I Pet. 2:9) which began with the believing "remnant according to the election of grace" (Rom. 11:5), to which the saved from among the Gentiles are added, according to the revelation of "the mystery," which God has now made known "unto His holy apostles and prophets by the Spirit, (namely) that *the Gentiles* should be fellow heirs, and of the same body," etc. (Eph. 3:1-6).

But even if we disregard the context and confine our attention to the verses quoted in the article we are reviewing, it is plain that they contain no prediction that the earthly Israel is to be "restored as a nation." The promise they contain is that Israel should *never cease from being a nation.* Now it is easy to see the fulfilment of this promise in Christ and His redeemed people; for "Israel" is perpetuated in that "peculiar people" (Tit. 2:14, I Pet. 2:9) just as David's line is maintained and perpetuated in Jesus Christ the Son of David risen from the dead (see also Mat. 21:43, where our Lord speaks of the new "nation"). But it is simply an impossibility that the prophecy that the seed of Israel should never "*cease from being a nation*" should apply to the natural seed of Jacob; for they *have* ceased from being a nation since the destruction of Jerusalem in A. D. 70.

Further the verses quoted from Jeremiah promised that God would not "cast off *all* the seed of Israel, for all that they have done." And God has *not* "cast off *all* the seed of Israel" – a fact which Paul is most careful to point out in Romans 11:1-5. For there we read that God "has not cast away His people *which He foreknew,*" but has accepted "the remnant according to the election of grace." And the apostle goes on to show in the same chapter, that these, with believing Gentiles "grafted in," constitute the "good olive tree," the true Israel of God.

In view of all this, which it needs no special gift of spiritual intelligence to discern, any one who cites Jeremiah 31 as a prophecy of the future restoration of the natural Israel as a nation is *bound to show clearly where that prediction is to be found in it.* But the article I am reviewing contains *not a word of explanation to that effect.* The writer thereof merely quotes along with it Jeremiah 33:25, 26 (where the prophet foretells, as he does in various other passages, the return of the Jews from the then approaching *Babylonian* captivity), and then makes the following comment:

> "Thanks, Jeremiah, we know that you have much more to say that was given you from the Lord; but this is to the point and quite sufficient."

And not a word of explanation does he give to show wherein the verses quoted from Jeremiah relate in any wise to the political status of the natural Israel in a yet future era. The writer of that article appears to have a very poor opinion of the intelligence of his readers.

EZEKIEL'S TESTIMONY

Next is quoted the following:

> "Thus saith the Lord God; Behold, I will take the children of Israel from among the heathen, whither they be gone" – they were already in captivity when this prophecy was given – "and will gather them on every side, and bring them into their own land: And I will make them one nation in the land upon the mountains of Israel; and one king shall be king to them all: and they shall be no more two nations, neither shall they be divided into two kingdoms any more at all" (Ezek. 37:21, 22).

The context of this prophecy makes it quite plain that it relates to the kingdom of Christ and the "everlasting covenant" (see particularly verses 24-26). The oneness here foretold is the oneness of all who are in Christ, "whether Jews or Gentiles" (1 Cor. 12:13; Gal. 3:28; Eph. 2:13-15; Col. 3-11). So it has always been understood by Christian teachers and commentators; and therefore anyone who now would put a radically different interpretation upon the passage is called upon to prove his case convincingly. The vision of Ezekiel 37 is one of a series which begins at chapter 34 with God's stern reproof of "the shepherds of Israel," in which chapter He makes the great promise, "*Behold, I, even I,* will both search My sheep, and seek them out" (37:11). This puts us on the right track for the true explanation of these prophecies. But again the writer completely ignores the context; and again he makes not the slightest attempt to show that the passage prophesies the restoration of Israel as an earthly people. Therefore we need not dwell longer upon it.

ISAIAH'S TESTIMONY

Then we have this passage:

"And He shall set up an ensign for the nations, and shall assemble the outcasts of Israel, and gather together the dispersed of Judah from the four corners of the earth. The envy also of Judah shall be cut off: Ephraim shall not envy Judah, and Judah shall not vex Ephraim" (Isa. 11:12, 13).

This Scripture is part of one of the most glorious of all the O. T. prophecies of Christ and His gospel; and I protest earnestly against the attempt to put upon it a meaning that would lend support to the carnal expectations of apostate Jews. The verses immediately preceding the quotation are these:

"In that day" – what day? – "there shall be a root of Jesse, which shall stand for an ensign of the people; and *to it shall the Gentiles seek:* and *His rest shall be glorious.* And it shall come to pass *in that day*, that the Lord shall set His hand the second time to recover *the remnant of His people* which shall be left from Assyria, and from Egypt" – etc. (comp. the countries out of which they were gathered on the day of Pentecost, Ac. 2:9-11) –

And then follow the words quoted in the article under consideration, viz., "And He shall set up *an ensign for the nations*" (*the Gentiles!*). So here we have a clear and distinct prophecy of the gospel, precisely as it was historically fulfilled in the beginning of this dispensation. Christ was to come as a "Shoot" or "Branch" out of the stem of Jesse (the royal house being cut down to the roots); and "the spirit of the Lord" was to "rest upon Him" (vv. 1, 2). This "Root of Jesse" was to stand for an ensign (a banner or standard) for the people; and *the Gentiles* were to seek unto Him; and He should bring them into a glorious rest (v. 10). And specifically, He should first "recover the remnant of His people" (v. 10), and then "set up an ensign for the nations." All of which has been gloriously fulfilled. And so wondrously do the historical facts correspond to the inspired prediction that very few, I am sure, even in this day of what has been not inaptly termed "crazy-quilt dispensationalism," would have the temerity to take this blessed prophecy away from the redeemed of the Lord and apply it to an earthly people of a yet future era.

And when we turn to the article where the above quoted verses are cited, in order to learn wherein they speak of the restoration of natural Israel as a nation in a yet future day, we find *no explanation at all*. It is simply taken for granted that the "king" (spelled with a small *k*) is a mortal man, and that the people are "Israel after the flesh" (I Cor. 10:18).

THE NEW TESTAMENT SCRIPTURES

Our writer now turns to the N. T. and quotes (or rather partly *mis*-quotes and partly garbles) the scripture which says that –

"Jesus Christ was a minister of the circumcision for the truth of God to confirm the promises made unto the fathers: *and that the Gentiles might glorify God for His mercy*" (Rom. 16:9).

The words I have italicized, which are a part of the same sentence with what precedes, are not quoted in the article at all; and the omission is highly significant, inasmuch as in this passage Paul, as "the minister of Jesus Christ *to the Gentiles*" (v. 16), is citing O. T. Scriptures to show what were *God's purposes and promises from of old concerning the Gentiles.* His promises in that regard began with the assurance given to Abraham that in his Seed should *all the nations of the earth be blessed* (Gen. 22:18). Those promises were renewed through Moses, David, and Isaiah, as the apostle in this passage sets forth. And *those* were "the promises made unto the fathers" that Christ came "to confirm." Yet the writer of the article we are reviewing ignores the perfectly plain sense of the passage, and takes it for granted, *first*, that God had promised the fathers of Israel that He would reconstitute that nation in a post-gospel era (whereas He promised no such thing, but the very opposite); and *second*, that Christ came to confirm *that* (purely imaginary) promise.

186

Surely the importance of the matter at issue demands at least a serious attempt to show that the Scriptures quoted lend support to the view advocated by the one who quotes them. But none is made in the paper now under review.

Following this is a very cursory reference to Romans 11, from which several short bits are quoted, and again with no explanation of the bearing of the quotations. It is my understanding of the matter, and in another chapter (Chap. XVII) I have attempted to show, that Romans 11 contains proof of the most conclusive sort that there is *no future in the purposes of God for the natural seed of Jacob as a nation,* but that there is the hope and promise of *personal salvation* for individual Israelites – 'if they abide not still in unbelief' (Rom. 11:23).

Lastly Acts 15:14-17 is quoted, and it is stated that the phrase "After this" means after this present gospel dispensation is ended. It matters little what era that phrase indicates, for the passage speaks *not a word* about restoring again the Jewish nation, but of raising up the tabernacle of David – a very different matter (see chapter herein on *The Tabernacle of David*). But the application which James makes of these words (quoted by him from Amos 9:11) shows plainly that the time indicated by the words "after this" was the time *then already come* when the convocation at Jerusalem was being held. A reference to the text and context (Am. 9:9-11) will abundantly confirm this.

Therefore, no other conclusion is possible from a careful examination of the Scriptures cited in the article we are discussing, than that the doctrine of a yet future restoration of the Jewish nation has not a scriptural leg to stand upon.

It would be, of course, a tedious business to examine minutely every passage in which old covenant shadows – as *Israel, Zion, Jerusalem, the temple,* etc. – are mentioned as symbols of the eternal realities they represent. Nor is there any need to do so in order to arrive at the truth of the matter we are investigating. A single plain statement of the New Testament will suffice for that. This, for example:

"Nevertheless, what saith the Scripture? Cast out the bondwoman and her son; for the son of the bondwoman shall not be heir with the son of the freewoman" (Gal. 4:30).

In this passage the apostle Paul not only "spiritualizes" the O. T. Scripture (as in fact he does habitually) but he also makes it certain that all the unfulfilled promises of God are for the *spiritual* seed of Abraham (Gal. 3:7, 29; see also Heb. 2:16, marg. and Lu. 1:54,55). This should put the matter beyond dispute for all who accept the epistles of Paul as the Word of God.

CHAPTER XX
CONCERNING THE MILLENNIUM

The millennium is a subject of fascinating interest. So little, however, is said about it in the Bible that almost boundless room is left to the imagination in respect to the details thereof; and it must be admitted that expositors have taken full advantage of the opportunities thus afforded.

All that is written on the subject is found in the first ten verses of Revelation, Chapter XX. As literally translated (following the text of *The Englishman's Greek N. T.* (Bagster) those verses read:

"And I saw an angel descending out of heaven having the key of the abyss and a great chain in his hand. And he laid hold of the dragon, the ancient serpent, who is the devil and Satan, and bound him *a thousand years*, and cast him into the abyss and shut him up and sealed over him, that he should not longer mislead the nations until *the thousand years* were completed; and after these things he must be loosed a little time.

"And I saw thrones, and they sat upon them, and judgment was given to them; and the souls of those that had been beheaded for the testimony of Jesus and on account of the word of God, and those that did not do homage to the beast, or his image, and did not receive the mark upon their forehead and upon their hand; and they lived and reigned with Christ *the thousand years*, but the rest of the dead lived not again (the critical texts all omit again) until *the thousand years* should have been completed. This is the first resurrection. Blessed and holy he who has part in the first resurrection. Over these the second death has no authority; but they shall be priests of God and of Christ and shall reign with him *a thousand years*. And when *the thousand years* may have been completed, Satan will be loosed out of his prison and will go out to mislead the nations which are in the four corners of the earth, Gog and

Magog to gather them unto war, of whom the number is as the sand of the sea. And they went up upon the breadth of the earth and encircled the camp of the saints and the beloved city. And there came down fire from God out of heaven and devoured them. And the devil who misleads them was cast into the lake of fire and brimstone where are the beast and the false prophet; and they shall be tormented day and night for the ages of the ages."

In the interpretation of the above passage, the principal question to be decided is: *in what realm* do the described events take place? Are they in the realm of *the natural*, or in that of the *spiritual*? They who locate them in the realm of the natural, in other words who make them a part of this earth's history, must of necessity postpone them to a future era, regardless of whether they place Christ's second coming before the millennium or after; for certainly no such events as are here described have as yet transpired on earth. But, for those who locate the scenes and events of the millennium in the realm of the unseen things, there is no such necessity. According to their understanding of the passage those scenes and events may be already past, or they may be going on now.

This preliminary question must be decided by the testimony of the passage itself; and to my mind its terms clearly indicate that the seer of Patmos is here describing events of the spiritual realm. For to begin with, the two actors in the first scene are *spiritual beings*; and since it must be that the "key" and the "great chain" are spiritual – not material – objects, and also that the place of Satan's confinement, called in the A. V. "the bottomless pit," but designated in the original text by the single and very expressive word, *abussos* (abyss), is a spiritual locality. Hence also the binding and the sealing of Satan are spiritual actions, corresponding to what those words describe in the realm of the natural.

Furthermore, in the second scene John saw *the souls* of those who *had been* (pluperfect tense) beheaded for the testimony of Jesus, together with those who did not receive the mark of the beast; and these all lived and reigned with Christ during the thousand years; from which it is evident that the passage has to do with things in the spiritual realm, where "the souls" of departed believers are now awaiting their resurrection bodies. It also indicates what is meant by "the first resurrection," as will be shown below.

HELP FROM THE RELATIVITY THEORY

The Einsteinian Relativity Theory posits a relationship between space and time of such nature as makes *time* to be a fourth dimension of *space*. In the current philosophical jargon this idea is expressed by the clumsy phrase, "*space-time continuum.*" According to this idea, one, should never speak of a *here*, or of a *now*, in his experience; for his *here* is never detached from his *now*. Hence, in the interest of accuracy, the proper expression is *here-now*.

As an illustration of what is involved in this view of *space-time*, we are reminded that a man's infancy and his old age are just as truly parts of himself as his head and his heels. In other words, it takes the full measure of the *time* he occupies as well as the full measure of the *space* he occupies, to make the complete individual.

That there is indeed some such relation between space and time seems evident when we reflect, in the light of the Scriptures upon *the Being of God*; for in that light we perceive that, just as God is everywhere present in space, even so He is everywhere present in time; that with Him there is no past and no future. God speaks habitually of things future as if they were present before Him; and so they undoubtedly are. We get this conception of God's Being and Nature from statements such as that He "inhabits eternity," and that with Him "one day is as a thousand years, and a thousand years as one day."

Applying this idea to the case of a prophecy whereof we know of no fulfilment, it is evident that we may do with it either of two things: (1) we may locate the fulfilment in another realm of space, or (2) we may locate it in another era of time. And specifically, we may either (1) assume its fulfillment to be in this realm of the natural and visible at a *future era of time*, or we may (2) assume its fulfilment to be at this present time (or in a time already past) in *another region of space*. The first of these alternatives is that which is usually chosen; the reason being that it is far easier for us to conceive of a future era of time where the same state of things with which we are familiar is still going on, than to conceive of a realm co-existent with this where a state of things of a spiritual kind subsists. Yet the latter explanation is obviously as satisfactory and sufficient as the former. And what we claim for it is that it has solid support in the Scripture; whereas the postponement of the prophecies concerning Israel, Zion and Jerusalem to a yet future era is contrary to clear statements of the word of God.

DR. STAFFORD'S STUDY OF THE KINGDOM

I have lately come upon an explanation of the passage we are now examining, which, because it takes full account of the facts noted above, and because also of its close adherence to the Scriptures and its rejection of all human imaginings, is the most satisfactory explanation of the millennium that has thus far come to my notice. It is found in *A Study of the Kingdom*, by Dr. T. P. Stafford (published by the Baptist Sunday School Board, Nashville, Tenn.).

In what follows I have made use of Dr. Stafford's explanation, at least as to all its most prominent features; for I had already become convinced from the evidence afforded by the passage itself that it pertains to the spiritual realm.

Dr. Stafford, after presenting his interpretation of the passage, makes the following statement, which to me is of much interest:

"Some years ago I thought out for myself this interpretation and the proof just cited. I thought I could claim originality for it. But to my chagrin I discovered the other day that Augustine made the same interpretation supported by the same words of Jesus (*City of God*, 20, 7). I cannot therefore, claim originality for the interpretation; but there is more assurance that it is sound."

Dr. Stafford points out (and it is important to take note of this) that the author of Revelation did not adopt or share in any degree whatever, the then current Jewish expectation of a millennium of Jewish ascendency over the Gentiles, and of world-wide peace and plenty And he quotes Adam Smith's *Life and Letters of St. Paul* to the effect that the early Christian imagination proceeded upon the Jewish notion that the history of the world was to last for six ages, corresponding to the six days of Creation. And that "just as the six days of creation were succeeded by a day of rest, so the six ages will be followed by the Millennium, a thousand years of peace. By and by the idea arose that each of the past ages had lasted a thousand years; and hence it was reckoned that the year 1000 A. D., would terminate the current age and witness the Lord's Advent, and the final Judgment."

As to this Dr. Stafford comments as follows:

"That there was a Jewish expectation of a millennium of some kind, and that it has had some influence upon Christian eschatology, is freely admitted. But that this Jewish notion is found in the New Testament is denied. This false idea, like many other false ideas, has come into Christian thought from Judaism, but does not belong there."

In proof of this Dr. Stafford points out that our Lord Himself was a martyr to His outspoken "nonconformity to Jewish notions," and to the fact that He was a complete contradiction to their ideas of the Messiah; "that Paul's life-long fight was against Jewish notions"; and that he "saved Christianity from the ruin which the Jewish party in the first churches would have brought upon it." And rightly he says: "The idea of a civil government on earth for a thousand years is not found in a single utterance of Jesus, Paul or Peter; much less that Christ is going to 'set it up' when He returns."

It is very significant indeed that, in the various passages that refer to Christ's second advent, although a number of things He will do are specified, *not a word is said about the setting up of a civil government on earth.* Indeed, as will be shown later on, some of the things that are definitely predicted to happen at that time, effectually exclude the possibility of the millennium which many are now expecting.

THE SECOND DEATH AND THE FIRST RESURRECTION

Looking to the passage itself for indications to guide us to a right understanding thereof, we note these antithetical statements: "This is the *first resurrection*," and "Over these *the second death* hath no authority" (vv. 5, 6). At verse 14, and again in verse 8 of the next chapter, it is explained that *the lake of fire is the second death.*

Here again we must face the question of interpreting the words of Scripture "literally." When, for example, Christ said, "This is my body," did He intend we should understand Him "literally?" Having dealt with this question elsewhere in this volume (See Chapter 11) I will only remind the reader that the prophets commonly employ figurative language, and that a distinctive characteristic of the Apocalypse is that it is written in the language of figures, signs and symbols. Dr. Stafford puts it thus (p. 229):

"In order that the symbol or figure of speech, that is, the saying of one thing and the meaning of another may be seen to be most common Revelation; and in order that the fact may be appreciated as essential to a proper interpretation of the prophecy I cite a number of examples, moving rapidly through the Book. In many cases the meaning is explained by John himself: 'The seven stars are the angels of the seven churches, and the seven candlesticks are the seven churches' (1:20). The Smyrna church is to have tribulation 'ten days' (2:10), which can hardly be taken with mathematical exactness. Satan's throne is said to be in Pergamum, that is, some great evil was there (2:13). 'The sword of my mouth,' a figure that occurs several times, means the truth of Christ (2:16. cf. 19:15, 21). 'Hidden manna' and white stone' stands for salvation or spiritual fellowship with Christ (2:17)......... Key of David' means the power of David; and 'David' here is not David, but David's Son, that is, the Son of God (3:17). 'Pillar in the temple of my God' means place of influence in the kingdom (3:12). Neither a literal (or material) pillar or temple is to be thought of. 'Door' does not mean *door*, but something spiritual analogous thereto. . . . . The robes of the saints are said to be made 'white in the blood of the Lamb' (7:14); but actual blood does not make garments white, and 'robes' here does not mean robes but souls, hearts, lives. . . . Some are to be 'tormented five months' (9:5, 10); but certainly 'five months' does not mean that measure of time."

And so on, giving several more pages of illustrations, without exhausting the instances contained in the Book.

Applying what is to be learned from these examples of the figurative use of words to the statement that the lake of fire is the second death, Dr. Stafford says:

"Of course he (John) does not mean that the lake of fire is itself the second death, but that being cast into it is, or signifies, the second death. We have here a valuable key, and we have the right to use it for all it is worth. What now *is* the second death? It is the eternal punishment to which the wicked and the unbelieving are doomed. John says so (20:10).

"If then eternal punishment is the second death, it follows that, in the conception of John as well as according to Biblical history, the *first* death is the banishment and punishment that came upon the race on account of the first sin: 'In the day that thou eatest thereof thou shalt surely die' (Gen. 2:17). John chose not to consider in this connection *physical* death, or else he counted it a part of the curse of the first death, which it is."

Thus it is made evident that John is here speaking of death in the spiritual sense; which is no new thing in the Bible, that being indeed the true sense of the word and the sense in which it is first used in the Bible (Gen. 2:17. See also John 5:24; 8:51; 11:25, 26; Rom. 5:4; 6:9; 8:6; Eph. 2:1, and many other passages). If then eternal banishment from the presence of God (2 Th. 2:9) is, in the terminology of the passage we are studying, "the second death," that fact directs us to the meaning of the antithetical statement, "This is the *first resurrection*"; for if the second death is not the death of the body, neither is the first resurrection the resurrection of the body.

According to the passage itself the first resurrection is sitting upon "thrones" and exercising "judgment"; it is living and reigning with Christ a thousand years. They who thus *lived* and reigned were *the souls* of those that had been beheaded on account of the testimony of Jesus, and also those who did not worship the beast or his image or receive his mark; and this includes, not the martyrs only, but all the saved; for verse 6 says, "Blessed and holy is he who has part in the first resurrection. Over these the second death has no authority; but they shall be priests of God and of Christ, and shall reign with Him a thousand years." The antithesis in this passage between "the first resurrection" and "the second death" makes it further evident that if the latter does not mean bodily death the former does not mean bodily resurrection.

It should be recalled in this connection that in the New Testament the unconverted are regarded as existing in a state of *death* and of servitude to *sin*. (Indeed the teaching of the Bible throughout is that death is not *the extinction* of man's being, but is *a state of being*.) At conversion man's natural condition is *reversed*; he *lives* and *reigns*. The first thing that happens is that he passes from death into life. This much of the doctrine is relatively easy to grasp; but more than that, instead of being, after conversion, under the rule and authority of sin, he himself shares the authority of Christ. He not only *lives with Him*, but also *reigns with Him*. That the N. T. clearly teaches this two-fold truth as to a man's change of condition at his conversion, will be clearly shown in what follows.

Further it will be shown that both the *living* with Christ and also the *reigning* with Him are *in another sphere*; not in the realm of the natural, but in that of the spiritual. Our *life* is not here; it is *hid* with Christ, in God (Col. 3:3). So likewise, our *reigning* is not here; for manifestly we are not seated on thrones in this life. But just as we live with and in our risen Lord in the heavenlies, so likewise do we reign with Him there and *now*. The fact that our true life is in the unseen world, while we continue here in the flesh, makes it easier to lay hold of the companion truth that our share in Christ's *royal authority*, as well as our share in His *resurrection life*, begins *when we believe in Him*. The moment one becomes a sharer of His life, that moment he becomes also a sharer of His throne. The N. T. clearly teaches this, as we shall see.

LIVING AND REIGNING WITH CHRIST

Two sayings of Christ Himself, both recorded by John in his Gospel, will help us settle the meaning of this passage. In John 5:24 we find the saying, "He that heareth My word, and believeth on Him that sent Me, *hath* everlasting life, and shall not come into condemnation (judgment); but is passed from (out of) *death* into *life*." Evidently the expressions *"hath everlasting life,"* and *"is passed . . into life"* are equivalent in meaning to *"they lived"*; and *"is passed out of death"* is equivalent to *"over these the second death hath no authority."* We conclude therefore, that those of whom Christ speaks in John 5:24 are they who have part in the first resurrection. In neither passage is bodily death or bodily resurrection in view at all.

Again, in John 11:25, 26 we find the saying of Jesus: *"I am the resurrection* and the life; he that believeth in Me though he were dead yet shall he live; and whosoever liveth and believeth in Me, shall never die." Here is a "resurrection" which is wholly apart from that of the body; and one that comes *before* that of the body. Hence this is plainly "the *first* resurrection"; and since *Christ Himself* is *this* resurrection, all His members, that is, all who believe in Him, have part therein. And manifestly, the statement, "He that *liveth* and believeth in Me shall *never die*," declares exactly the same truth as the words "They lived over these *the second death* has no authority."

It is confirmatory of the view we are advocating that the writer of the Apocalypse shows, by what he had written in his Gospel, that he had learned from his Master of a "resurrection" which preceded the resurrection of the body, and which hence was, with respect thereto, *"the first* resurrection." Personally I feel, in the light of these Scriptures, quite clear as to the meaning of the phrase, "the first resurrection') in Revelation XX.

THE TESTIMONY OF PAUL

Yet there is more, and equally strong, confirmation in the writings of Paul; for that apostle refers time and again to a resurrection which is the experience of those who have not yet experienced bodily death and resurrection, and which therefore is, relatively to the latter, "the *first* resurrection." We read that God "hath quickened us together with Christ . . . and hath *raised us up together*" &c. (Eph. 2:5, 6); and again, "Buried with Him in baptism, wherein also ye are *risen with Him* through faith" (Col. 2:12); and again, "If ye then be *risen with Christ*, seek those things which are above, where Christ sitteth" (i.e. on a throne; Col. 3:1). Paul repeatedly speaks of believers as those that are *alive from the dead*; and he teaches that they should yield themselves unto God "as those that are alive from the dead" (Rom. 6:13).

The passage in Ephesians is specially pertinent and illuminating, and it merits therefore, our closest attention. In chapter I, Paul expresses the earnestness of his desire and prayer that the converts at Ephesus might come to know the exceeding greatness of God's power toward us *who believe* (reminding us of Christ's word to Martha, "lie that *believeth* in Me"), which is "according to the working of His mighty power which He wrought in Christ when He *raised Him from the dead* and set Him (*i. e. on a throne*) at His own right hand in the heavenlies" etc. (vv. 19-22). Then in Chapter 11 the apostle plainly declares the truth he so intensely desired them to "know," saying that God, "for His great love wherewith He loved us, even when we were *dead* in sins (spiritually dead), *hath quickened us together with Christ* (by grace ye are saved) and *hath raised us up together*, and made us *sit together* (on thrones) in the heavenlies" (vv. 4-6).

Here is a close parallel to what John saw, in the vision described in the passage we are studying, beginning, "And I saw thrones, and *they sat* upon them," answering to which Paul tells us that we, who are saved by grace are even now *seated on thrones* in the heavenly places. The words "*hath quickened us together with Christ . . and made us sit together*," in the one passage, are the equivalent in meaning of "they *lived* and *reigned* (together) *with Christ*," in the other; and the words, "hath raised us up together," are equivalent in meaning to, "this is the first resurrection."

Paul uses the expression "the heavenly places" to designate what I have referred to as "the realm of the spiritual." The expression occurs five times in Ephesians. The last occurrence is rendered in our A. V. *"high places"* (Eph. 6:12). That passage speaks definitely of the conflict we are now waging with the hosts of *"spiritual wickedness"* in those heavenly places; which shows that Satan's servants are there. Peter designates that same realm, "Zion" (I P. 2:6; see also Heb. 12:22).

Again "Paul writes: "For though we walk in the flesh we do not war after the flesh. For the weapons of our warfare are not carnal, but (they are) mighty through God to the pulling down of strongholds" (2 Cor. 10:3, 4). We often read these statements, but we fail to grasp their full meaning. The things of the flesh seem real and substantial, while those of the spirit seem unreal, remote and shadowy. Hence we fail to realize that in truth it is just the other way.

Referring to some of the Scriptures quoted above, Dr. Stafford says:

"That the Christian life is *a spiritual resurrection,* and that unsaved people are *spiritually dead* are common conceptions with Paul and John. (Cf. Col. 3:1; Rom. 6:4; John 5:21, 24; 6:54; 10:10; 17:23; 1 Jno. 5:13; Rom. 6:23; Eph. 2:1).

"That Christians sit upon thrones as Christ does, (or that they reign as Christ does) is a common conception in the N. T. Christ sits upon a spiritual throne and so do they. Christ reigns by moral and spiritual influence, and so do they. This is not something that is yet to be. This has been going on since the death and the exaltation of Christ, which was His enthronement. He Himself originated both the thought and also this use of the imagery, it seems (Mat. 19:28). As Abraham, Isaac and Jacob have prominence in the kingdom of God, so have the apostles. In that sense they sit on thrones and reign. And in the same sense all Christians sit on thrones and reign Paul the thirteenth apostle reigns as do the others. Jesus said to His disciples: 'Ye are the salt of the earth.' We all understand that statement. Well, that is reigning morally and spiritually. That kind of reigning will satisfy every Christian that is not ambitious and mean. Every moral and spiritual blessing that has come to the

199

world in nineteen centuries has come from Christ and His people. That is reigning. Every cleansing fire that has burned out the impurities of society has come from Christ and His people. That is the dispensing of judgment. All seriously-minded and thoughtful people know that the only hope of the world is the gospel of Christ, which His real followers, and they only, proclaim. That is world-dominion; the only sort that we, as Christians, should desire. So Jesus says, 'He that overcometh, I will give to him *to sit down with me in my throne*, as I also overcame and sat down with my Father in His throne (Rev. 3:21). It is in this book of Revelation that God's people are described as 'a kingdom and priests' (5:10). So also in the passage we are dealing with it is written: 'They shall be priests of God and of Christ, and shall reign with Him' (cf. 1 Pet. 2:9)."

Particularly it is to be noted in this connection that the special business and responsibility of a King is to *save*. As God, speaking to Israel through the prophet Hosea, says: "O Israel, thou hast destroyed thyself; but in me is thy help. I will be *thy King*. Where is any other that may *save thee* in all thy cities?" (Hos. 13:9, 10). When therefore, any of Christ's people take part in the salvation of sinners, they are engaged in what is preeminently a kingly business; and in so doing they reign with Christ.

It is much easier to understand how Christians exercise the office of priests than how they exercise that of kings. As says Dr. Stafford:

"How Christians are priests we understand quite well. It means that every Christian has direct access to Christ and God. It means that they are persons through whom God mediates to the world His salvation. When it is said that Christians are *priests*, we do not think of robes, and bells, and candles, and ceremonial performances. That is, evangelical Christians and most Protestants do not. Why do we not apply the same good sense to the Bible when it speaks of Christians as *on thrones* and *reigning*? But many think immediately of literal thrones and golden crowns. The whole trouble is with our thinking."

Surely, if Christ's people are "priests unto God," and if they exercise the office of priests in a strictly spiritual sense, and without anything in their appearance, their circumstances or their actions to indicate it, we must needs conclude that they are kings also, and exercise the functions of kings, in a strictly spiritual sense; it being understood that by "spiritual" is not meant *unreal*, but *just the reverse*.

Dr. Stafford reminds us that a king, of the sort we are acquainted with, was never God's plan for His people. He "gave them a king in His anger" (Hos. 13: 11); and when they demanded of Him a king, He sent thunder and rain in harvest season (when it never occurs in Palestine), in order, as Samuel declared to them, "that ye may perceive and see that your wickedness is great which ye have done in the sight of the Lord, *in asking you a king*" (1 Sam. 12:12-18). As says Dr. Stafford:

> "The king business, like the priest business, belongs to the tutelage of the race. It is a thing of the past, not of the future. And yet many associate the golden age of the world with actual kings [such as we are acquainted with] and thrones and all the accompanying regalia and paraphernalia. . . . Imagine me, for example, sitting on a literal throne somewhere, say on the Mount of Olives! But every other Christian is sitting on a little throne too. There would not be room enough on the Mount of Olives, or indeed in all Palestine, to plant our thrones. There we all sit, with shining crowns, flourishing our golden sceptres, and not a subject to black our boots. I abdicate my throne right now."

SATAN BOUND AND LOOSED

In verses 1-3 John describes the coming down from heaven of a mighty angel, who lays hold upon the Devil, and binds him and casts him into the bottomless pit, "till the thousand years should be fulfilled," after which "he must be loosed a little season"; and verse 7 says: "And when the thousand years are expired, Satan shall be loosed out of his prison."

As Dr. Stafford says: "We must regard this as either a complete or a partial depriving of Satan of his power." And he goes on to say:

"It must for two reasons be the latter: "The first reason is that the complete stripping of Satan of his power follows in our text (Rev. XX) immediately after this limitation of his power. The severer and the final judgment and punishment are described in verse 10. The preceding binding of Satan was therefore something less than a complete taking-away of his power.

"The second reason is that Christ Himself, when He was on earth, bound Satan. He said so: 'How can one enter into the strong man's house, and seize his goods,' He asked, 'except he first *bind the strong man?*' (Mat. 12:29). The strong man is Satan. The stronger than he, who binds him, is Jesus. "But Satan is not so bound as to have no power at all. It is a *limiting* of his power, a circumscribing of his influence and activities that is meant."

A passage in Hebrews will help us at this point:

"For as much then as the children are partakers of flesh and blood, He also Himself likewise took part of the same; that through death He might destroy *him that had the power of death that is the Devil, and deliver them who through fear of death were all their lifetime subject to bondage*" (Heb. 2:14, 15).

This clearly refers to the same truth as that declared by Christ in Matthew 12:29; for the one whose power was destroyed by Jesus is expressly said to be "the Devil," and those who are delivered from his power, "the children," are "the goods" of which Jesus, by His death, has despoiled him. It is evident too, that "destroy him" does not mean the complete deprivation of his power, for he still exercises the power of death, and on a large scale; but it means the crippling and limiting of that power, which Satan can now exercise only on those who believe not.

The above is in full agreement with the words of Christ to the seventy, when they returned to Him with joy, saying, "Lord, even the devils are subject unto us through thy Name. And He said unto

202

them, I beheld Satan as lightning fall from heaven. Behold, I give you power to tread on serpents and scorpions, and *over all the power of the enemy*" (Lu. 10:19). Here was a binding of Satan, in that his power was greatly restricted.

In John's vision the binding of Satan was done by the instrumentality of an angel from heaven; and by the passage in Hebrews we learn that the effective cause of the breaking of his power was *the death* of Jesus Christ. It is pertinent therefore to recall that, on the morning of His resurrection, "the angel of the Lord descended from heaven, and came and rolled back the stone from the door" (Mat. 28:2). There is a suggestive correspondence between the action of opening the door of the tomb of the Lord Jesus, rolling away the great stone by means of which His body had been sealed therein, and the action of shutting Satan up in the abyss and setting a seal upon him. It suggests that both actions were performed by the same mighty angel and at the same time.

Again quoting from Dr. Stafford:

"That Satan's power is greatly limited in the Christian age but not wholly destroyed is certainly the fact. Consider that Jesus said as He approached His death on the cross, '*Now is the prince of this world cast out*' (Jno. 12:31. Cf. 16:11). But He did not cast him out in every sense; for He said afterward, 'The prince of this world cometh and hath nothing in Me' (Jno. 14:30). Here are conceptions of the limiting of Satan, or the casting out of Satan, that should guide us in interpreting Rev. 20:1-3. There ought to be no doubt at all as to the soundness and safety of this method of procedure.

"If now we have reasoned correctly up to this point, it is easy to say what 'the thousand years' signifies. It is *the Christian age,* extending up to a little time before Christ comes again. 'The thousand years, have become nearly two thousand years. Or are we now in 'the little time' that follows that period? I do not know [though the late war and its consequences make it seem likely]. But this is certain: *We are either in the millennium, or we have passed through it and we have entered the 'little time,' when from all quarters attacks are made on the very citadel of Christianity itself."*

Whether or not Dr. Stafford's explanation of this very difficult passage of Scripture is in all essential particulars correct, the present writer feels constrained to say concerning it, that on the one hand, it has more scriptural evidence in its favor than any other explanation of the passage that has come to the writer's knowledge up to now; whereas, on the other hand, he knows of nothing in the Scriptures that contradicts it.

And whatever be the true sense and meaning of the passage, it certainly lends not the slightest support to the doctrine of the restoration of the Jewish nation in a coming age and its exaltation to the position of lordship over the nations of the world.

The End

PHILIP MAURO
1859-1952

Philip Mauro was a lawyer who practiced before the Supreme Court and also a writer of Christian literature. As far as twentieth century Christian figures are concerned, Philip Mauro stands out as one of the most captivating. After coming to a saving knowledge of the Lord in 1903, at the age of forty five, Mauro, a member of the bar of the Supreme Court of the United States and one of the foremost patent lawyers of his day, began his "Testimony" of what was to him the most important event in his life.

His repeated successes in courts of law, coupled with his legal briefs, could not but gain recognition, for they were "models of accuracy, conciseness, and literary finish." As such, they were "frequently used by judges in the text of their decisions." Perhaps one of the most important occasions where his legal work was requisitioned was in connection with the famous Tennessee-Scopes trial in 1925. The argument which William Jennings Bryan used, and thereby won the case, was prepared by Philip Mauro.

His early twentieth century was a period of great expansion for many errors, such as Dispensationalism and Anglo Israelism. Mauro's book, "The Hope of Israel," which was written three years prior to the Scopes trial, stands as a testament to his astute mind and sharp pen, most dashing in the face of the most formidable adversaries. Rising to the forefront of Christianity's great struggle against these foes, he applied the preparation God had given him, and scored great victories for sound doctrine.

"We thus learn that the things prepared by God for the coming age, which are "for our glory," are "spiritual things." And not only are they spiritual things, but they are communicated by means of "spiritual words"; and they must be "spiritually discerned" (*God's Pilgrims*)

His works include *God's Pilgrims, The Church, The Churches and the Kingdom, The Hope of Israel, Ruth, The Satisfied Stranger, The Wonders of Bible Chronology, The Last Call to the Godly Remnant, More Than a Prophet, Dispensationalism Justifies the Crucifixion* and *Things Which Soon Must Come to Pass.*

Biographic information taken from:

Wikipedia

http://www.preteristarchive.com/StudyArchive/m/mauro-philip.html

23929207R00119

Printed in Poland
by Amazon Fulfillment
Poland Sp. z o.o., Wrocław